DATE DUE			
Feb 2 '70			
Jun 8 70			
Oct 28 73			
Jul 26 '74			
Jun 9 '75			
Jan 21 '76			
May 17 '76			
Sep 27 '76			
REN May '77			
REN May 7 8			
GAYLORD M-2			PRINTED IN U.S.A.

THE LITERARY CRITICISM OF
"YOUNG AMERICA"

THE LITERARY CRITICISM
OF "YOUNG AMERICA"

A Study in the Relationship of
Politics and Literature

1837-1850

By John Stafford

NEW YORK / RUSSELL & RUSSELL

University of California Publications
English Studies: 3

810.9

St 1 L

63616

November, 1968

ACKNOWLEDGMENTS

IN PREPARING this account of the literary criticism of "Young America," I have been helped by many scholars, librarians, and editors. My indebtedness to published studies is acknowledged in the text and notes, but my gratitude to those who assisted and encouraged me directly and personally must be acknowledged in this inadequate note.

I wish to thank Theodore Hornberger and Henry Nash Smith, under whose stimulation and guidance my study of the history of American literary criticism was begun.

To the Board of Editors of the series in which this monograph appears I owe more than the usual debt of gratitude. I thank them for their unselfish contributions of time and intelligence.

I should like also to express my gratitude for the assistance given me by the staffs of the libraries of the University of Texas and the University of California, Los Angeles, the public libraries of New York and Los Angeles, the library of the New-York Historical Society, and the Henry E. Huntington Library and Art Gallery.

I am indebted also to the financial assistance granted me by the Committee on Research of the Academic Senate of the University of California (Southern Section), and to the help of Arthur M. Sanderson and my other research assistants.

I wish finally to thank Mr. Glenn Gosling and Mr. Harold A. Small, of the University of California Press, for their careful editorial work.
                                                                    J. S.

CONTENTS

CHAPTER I

POLITICS, MAGAZINES, AND PUBLISHING

I

RALPH WALDO EMERSON observed that in intellectual and social history "there are always two parties, the party of the Past and the party of the Future; the Establishment and the Movement." At times, he added, the battle between the two becomes animated; "the schism runs under the world and appears in Literature, Philosophy, Church, State and social customs."[1] One such time of vigorous activity in the history of American literary criticism may be observed in the years from 1835 to 1850. The schism that showed itself in literary thought can be seen running through philosophy, church, and state also. This breach between Establishment and Movement was most open to view in the New York political periodicals of the post-Jackson era. In such periodicals as the *New York Review,* the *Whig Review* (the *American Review*), and the *Democratic Review* the party of the past and the party of the future made their opposition most explicit, showed most clearly the connection between literature and politics.

One group of New York critics writing for these reviews aligned itself unmistakably with the Movement party and, indeed, forced the issues that animated the battle. In the eighteen-forties this group came to be known by the appropriate name "Young America," a term probably originated by its most effervescent member, Cornelius Mathews, and perpetuated partly by its conservative enemies. Young America's leading members— Evert A. Duyckinck, William A. Jones, John L. O'Sullivan, and Parke Godwin—were well known in their day as vociferous advocates of a new and democratic American literature, a literature that would express the spirit of a young America, which they felt was manifestly destined to carry democracy to the rest of the world. Politically the leading Young Americans were Locofocos, that is, members of the liberal and radical wing of the Democratic Party, and their chief organ was the *Democratic Review,* in which they developed what Longfellow scornfully called a "Loco-foco politico-literary system." Though it may be granted that such representatives of the Establishment as Poe and, to use Young America's phrase, the "literary tories" of the *North American Review* wrote much of the best criticism of the day, yet the liberal, democratic Young Americans also wrote a respectable body of criticism: their critical judgments stand up remarkably well today—better than those of most other critics of their time.

II

To understand the "Loco-foco politico-literary system" of Young America, we must first glance at the political and social situation surrounding the group in New York. What was the Movement party, the Democratic Party, with which Young America was identified?

The most important characteristic of New York political life between 1835 and 1850 was the struggle between the radical, Jacksonian Democrats, called Locofocos after 1835, and the conservative Democrats and Whigs. The strife within the Democratic Party led to the formation by 1845 of three factions in New York: the conservative "Old Hunkers," the left-center "Young Hickories," and the antislavery "Barnburners." Young Americans were usually Young Hickories; for example, they edited and wrote for the New York *Morning News,* a newspaper referred to in 1845 as "a genteel young Democrat," which "represents the ambitious 'centre' of the Tammany Party."[2]

In the years following 1837 President Martin Van Buren converted the New York Locofoco policies into a national program, and the Democratic Party, especially the Northern wing, became popularly known as the Locofoco Party (hence Hawthorne, the "Locofoco Surveyor"). After choosing to go along with the radical wing of the party in 1837, Van Buren and his associates established a "high-class magazine, the *Democratic Review* ... which became an effective vehicle for the dissemination of the larger Loco-Focoism."[3] And it became in literary affairs the chief organ of the Young Americans.

The political and social philosophy of the Locofoco Democrats, who were ascendant in national politics through most of the years from 1837 to 1850, was one which owed much to its roots in the earlier New York Workingmen's Party: the Locofoco "philosophy, in truth, was that of a nascent proletarianism."[4] It was a philosophy which made the Democratic Party the party of the laboring man, the farmer, the "small man," the "people," as opposed to the Whig Party, which was, generally speaking, the party of the manufacturing interests, "big business," the "aristocracy." The Locofoco and Jacksonian Democrats went back to the earlier Jeffersonian doctrines for the basis of their beliefs. Their philosophy of Equal Rights was one which permitted them to discern a fundamental conflict·between the business community and farmers and laborers. "The people," farmers and laborers, as represented by the Democratic Party, should resist all attempts to concentrate power in the hands of a small group or class. Orestes A. Brownson summarized, "A Loco-foco is a Jeffersonian Democrat, who having realized political equality, passed through one phase of the revolution, now passes on to another, and attempts the realization of social equality, so that the actual condition of men in society shall be in harmony with their acknowledged rights as citizens."[5]

In meeting the specific political problems of the time, the Locofocos encouraged labor unions, continued the long Jacksonian war on the banking interests (which were held to be the

bulwarks of privilege), fought against monopoly and imprison-
ment for debt and for equal universal education, and in general
espoused any cause which seemed likely to lead to "the greatest
good of the greatest number."

The Establishment party, the Whig Party, began with the
assumption that society was best organized when those who had
the largest stake in society, the largest amount of property, were
in power. Under the pressure of changing conditions, largest of
which was probably the Democratic successes, the Whigs gradually changed their expressed political principles in the direction
of minimizing the differences between the interests of the classes,
between the interests of the rich and poor. The log cabin and
hard cider campaign of 1840 is symptomatic; the *Democratic
Review* remarked that the Whigs "have at last learned from
defeat the very art of victory! We have taught them how to con-
quer us!...They are now, forsooth, the 'Democratic Whigs'...."[6]

When applied to specific problems the Whig doctrines led to
opposition to changes in the banking laws, to labor organiza-
tions, and to the other reforms proposed by the Locofocos.

The most important organs in New York for the dissemination of the Whig philosophy and program were the *New York
Review* and later the *Whig Review,* which was set up frankly in
imitation of the *Democratic Review*. The *Whig Review*'s "Prospectus" commended the rival party's magazine for its ability but
objected to the many "pernicious doctrines" that it maintained:
the *Whig Review* would support the true doctrines of the party
which "is in all things essentially conservative, and at the same
time is the party of progress and improvement."[7]

III

Just as the literary criticism of Young America was influenced
directly by the political situation, it was also determined partly
by the periodicals for which it was written. Young America pub-

lished criticism in nearly every important magazine of the day, but the best and most influential of the magazines which it wrote for and one which it dominated was the *Democratic Review*. In the "passionless personage" of the *Democratic* we see in exaggerated outline the close connection between politics and literature in this period of American history.

The *Democratic Review* was founded in 1837 by two of the most political and least literary of the Young Americans, John L. O'Sullivan and his brother-in-law Samuel D. Langtree, two "very young, very sanguine, and very democratic" Irishmen. They were among the radical intellectuals of the country who were concerned because the "anti-democratic cause" possessed "at least two-thirds of the press of the country"; they saw that the respectable magazines—the *North American Review*, the *American Quarterly*, the *New England Magazine*, the recently established *New York Review*—were in the hands of the Whigs. They founded the *Democratic Review* to give liberal and radical intellectuals a voice and to promote a democratic American literature.[8]

First established in Washington, later moved to New York, the new journal won support from high places: O'Sullivan reported that "Old General Jackson took a great deal of interest in it, and was its first subscriber"; Attorney General Benjamin F. Butler was the most active "political friend" of the new magazine; Henry D. Gilpin, then a solicitor in the Treasury Department, later Attorney General, helped in the search for backing. One of the irrepressible Irish editors even approached John Quincy Adams, who, as Adams reported in his *Memoirs*, did *not* support the venture: "Long evening visit from Mr. Langtree—a fulsome flatterer. He urged me to write for his Democratic Review and Magazine; but I told him that literature was, and in its nature must always be, aristocratic; that democracy of numbers and literature were self-contradictory."[9]

From 1837 to 1841 Langtree and O'Sullivan were the editors, singly or in collaboration; from 1841 until at least the end of 1845 O'Sullivan was the sole editor. While O'Sullivan was gone to London on a diplomatic mission at the end of 1845, it is quite probable that Evert A. Duyckinck and William A. Jones, two other Young Americans, took charge of the *Democratic* as acting editors. At any rate Duyckinck became literary editor in early 1845, and on July 6, 1845, O'Sullivan tried, probably unsuccessfully, to sell him a half-interest in the magazine.[10] Early in 1846 the *Democratic* passed out of the direct control of the Young Americans, though their work continued to appear in it from time to time.

The magazine under Langtree and O'Sullivan was, according to the classification set up by the *Broadway Journal,* a first-of-the-month, five-dollar, New York, male, hundred-page, brown-covered magazine (as distinguished from the middle-of-the-month, three-dollar, Philadelphia, bisexual, pink-covered magazines). Its circulation probably averaged about thirty-five hundred during the years before 1850. Figures given in the preface to the *Review* for 1840 indicate an average of four or five thousand up to that date; in 1843 O'Sullivan claimed thirty-five hundred, and in 1845 about two thousand *subscribers.* The subscribers must have represented a relatively broad segment of society; C. A. Bristed said that it was one openly partisan review that "while it contained and paid for good articles, was subscribed to and even written for by many Whigs."[11] But even with its broad appeal it was too weighty to approach the mass circulation of the lighter magazines.

The editors started out paying well for contributions. Before the first number appeared, the editors wrote Hawthorne that the compensation "will be on so liberal a scale as to command the best and most polished exertions" of good writers: a minimum of three dollars and as much as five dollars per page. The sanguine editors were soon paying less. John Bigelow got only two or two and a half dollars per page in 1842; in 1843 Hawthorne was being paid only twenty dollars "for an article of what length soever," when dilatory payments did come to him; in 1843 Thoreau reported that it could afford only half or quarter pay, which, he added, "it *will* do."[12] Despite the financial hazards of publishing, the *Democratic* was paying well throughout its. career, by comparison, at least, with other journals of the time. The critics who wrote for it could afford to write serious criticism, and, since it was paying for creative works, the critics and editors were less tempted than many of the time to pay its writers in critical praise.

In form and content the *Democratic Review* was an interesting combination. As a concession to the "spirit of the age" (to use a Democratic catch phrase of the time), it did not retain the classic quarterly review form. But it did not swing completely over to the popular magazine form, as represented by *Graham's* and others: Young America believed that the public could safely reach a "few higher rungs" of the "intellectual ladder," "a little farther range of vision than the old poppy field" of *Godey's* and *Graham's.*[13] Its full name was significantly the *United States Magazine and Democratic Review,* a magazine and a review. Like other magazines it appeared monthly and contained original poems, short stories, and "sketches." Like other reviews it contained longer articles which used books as starting points. The success of this formula in meeting at least halfway the rising democratic mass market is seen in the flattery of the Whigs in setting up their review on the same pattern in 1845.

A glance at the *Democratic Review* for July, 1844, will perhaps make clear the type of its reading matter and the relative amount of space it gave to criticism. Opening with an engraving of Democrat James Fenimore Cooper, the number continues with an article on Van Buren, probably by O'Sullivan, a poem of

Victor Hugo's, an article on Texas, probably by A. H. Everett, a sixteen-page discussion of transcendentalism, and a story by Hawthorne. The ubiquitous magazine writer Henry T. Tuckerman next attempts to "breathe a strain" of poetry "whose tone may wake *an echo in thy heart,*" and Mrs. E. F. Ellet contributes a translation of a story by Eugène Sue. Following a poem by Goethe, William A. Jones reviews Horne's *New Spirit of the Age* and an unknown contributor discusses the "Influence of European on Asiatic Civilization." The *Review* proudly points out that the next selection is the first publication "on either side of the ocean" of Elizabeth Barrett's "Drama of Exile." Young American associate J. T. Headley describes the government of Rome and the Papal States in the next article, which is followed by "Work" and "Summer Love," poems by Elizabeth Barrett and "C." of "Concord, Mass." The number closes with a short article on Persico's new statue of Columbus in Washington, its usual "Monthly Financial and Commercial Article," "New Books," "Monthly Literary Bulletin," and one of the occasionally published reports on the meetings of the New York Historical Society.

O'Sullivan's taste is evident in the editorial supervision of the contents of the magazine before 1846. Fellow Young American William A. Jones praised his "catholicism of taste," his "liberality in laying the fewest possible restrictions on ... contributors, and confining the range of prohibited topics to the smallest possible circle."[14] Signed articles were probably not much tampered with, but unsigned articles and reviews suffered more. Often the editorial changes were without other than Procrustean motives, as when Emerson's notice of young Channing's poems was extended into puffery. Emerson begged Thoreau to tell William Emerson that the review had been "interpolated with sentences and extracts, to make it long, by the editor, and I acknowledge, as far as I remember, little beyond the first page."[15] But Emerson's name, it should be added, was not used on the review. In the field of politics, of course, the editorial supervision was undoubtedly quite rigid, and the views of the liberal or radical wing of the party were always dominant before 1846. The fate of one of Thoreau's articles is perhaps typical; he wrote Emerson that the *Review* had refused to accept his now famous article on Etzler's book but had asked for other matter, "purely literary, I suppose": "O'Sullivan wrote me that articles of this kind have to be referred to the circle who, it seems, are represented by this journal, and said something about 'collective we' and 'homogeneity.'" In writing to his mother of the same incident he said that the *Review* could not "adopt the sentiments," but "they were very polite, and earnest that I should send them something else, or reform that." On this occasion Thoreau bowed to the "collective we," for a month later he wrote Emerson that "O'Sullivan is printing the manuscript I sent him some time ago, having objected only to my want of sympathy with the Communities."[16] But the general policy of the editors was not so much a negative one of repression as a positive one of attracting writers who were naturally sympathetic to the program of the Democratic Party in politics and literature.

Though many of the milder Whigs might write for and subscribe to the *Democratic Review*, the more thoroughly conservative, respectable people, especially those around Boston, saw it and most Young Americans as horrifyingly radical. George Sumner's report of the reaction to his article on Greece is instructive: "because that article appeared in the Democratic Review, it is trodden under foot, and I am denounced as 'an Administration man.'" Nathan Hale refused to reprint the article in his newspaper; Ticknor "was sorry to see it in such company"; his brother Charles Sumner advised him to abandon his "leaky craft"; Professor Greenleaf was grieved; and Justice Story was troubled by his position, but "out of delicacy" would not mention it to his brother. George Sumner's response was radical enough: "God *damn* them all!! and yet I cannot but laugh, roars of horrid laughter, on thinking of all these things."[17]

The liberal and radical political program of the *Democratic* was reflected directly in the literary criticism of the magazine. It helped to determine the point of view in many general critical articles, leading to an interest in "poetry for the people," "literature for the million." And it influenced even the treatment of particular writers: Bryant, Whittier, Ebenezer Elliott, and other "people's poets," for example, received high praise. In short, the *Democratic Review* was the chief exponent of the Locofoco politico-literary system that Longfellow complained about.

Criticism was also made to serve more immediate, practical, political and economic ends, such as that of helping to win a political appointment for Hawthorne. On March 21, 1845, O'Sullivan wrote to Hawthorne that he had been urging Bancroft to give Hawthorne the Salem Post Office, or a consulship at Marseilles or Genoa or Gibraltar or Pekin. He continued: "For the purpose of presenting you more advantageously I have got Duyckinck to write an article about you in the April Democratic ... By manufacturing you thus into a Personage, I want to raise your mark higher in Polk's appreciation."[18] Thus did Young Americans Duyckinck and O'Sullivan serve politics and literature in the *Democratic Review*.

Two other distinguishing marks of the *Democratic* will become clearer as we look more closely at Young America. Under O'Sullivan and the other Young Americans it was always one of the strongest proponents of a democratic national literature (as opposed to the *Whig Review*'s advocacy of an aristocratic English literature). And it was generally sympathetic toward its fellow radicals in philosophy and literature, the New England transcendentalists. Lowell's comment on Young America's short-lived *Arcturus* might also be applied to the *Democratic*: it was "as transcendental as Gotham *can* be."[19]

The *Democratic*'s devotion to the younger and newer American writers, its relatively free and live intellectual qualities, made it one of the best periodicals of the time; while it was under the direction of Young America it was probably the best. Whitman, who wrote for it and agreed with its radical policies, spoke of it in 1858 as a "monthly magazine of a profounder quality of talent than any since," and added that in the early 'forties it "was largely impressing the public, especially the young men." In 1843, Poe, who could not agree with its policies, wrote: "Were it not for its ultraism in politics, we should consider the *Democratic Review* the most valuable journal of the day." Even before he contributed to it, he commended especially the "department of Criticism," which has "generally been conducted in a candid, sensible, and upright manner." George Parsons Lathrop called it "the most brilliant periodical of the time," and more recently F. L. Mott states that Lathrop is "perhaps right" for the years from 1836 to 1846.[20] Young America's editing of the *Democratic Review* was in itself a noteworthy contribution to American literary criticism.

IV

The literary criticism of Young America was directly influenced by a third development in the years between 1835 and 1850: by 1849 even the *Whig Review* was saying that "literature has gone over to the people."[21] If the years from 1830 to 1850 may be described by the historian as the period of the "rise of the common man," one of the most important developments in the literary and publishing life of the nation may be described in similar terms: the years leading up to 1850 saw the rise of the common reader. Advances in publishing and bookselling methods made it possible for a large share of the common people to buy books; by a process in which cause and effect are indistinguishable the wide reading audience then provoked further changes in bookselling and publishing. The whole cycle had a profound influence on literature and literary criticism.

It was an influence playing mainly into the hands of the Movement party and Young America, for it tended to change, to
democratize, literature. The mechanical improvements which
permitted the mass production of books helped create the publishing *business,* which needed advertising to dispose of its
products. Enterprising publishers adopted many means of "advertising" their books by assuring a good critical reception for
them. And the extensive circulation of English and (despite the
lack of an international copyright law) American books contributed to the rise of the professional author in America and,
incidentally, created a new situation in which the critic had to
work. The critic, especially the Young American critic, could
find many American authors and American books to praise; he
could appeal to the "reading democracy" in their behalf.

As the first influence on Young America's criticism, we may
notice that the rapid industrialization made possible by the new
techniques in printing in the first half of the nineteenth century
had the usual centralizing effect: the larger cities, especially New
York and Philadelphia, became publishing centers. And the
New York of Young America's day was somewhat more important as a publishing center than was Philadelphia, a fact
which helps to explain the wide influence of Young America
and its hardheaded understanding of the significance of the new
methods of commercial or democratic patronage for literature.[22]

The new publishing economy underlies a second aspect of
Young America's criticism: the mass production of cheap books
created a new kind of market, a new audience, and changed the
task of the critic.[23] An anonymous *Democratic Review* writer
(who sounds like a Young American) in 1848 estimated the
number of readers and speculated on its implications. In 1802,
he began, there were ten million people in England and four
million in the United States; of these there were probably one
million readers, all aristocratic, in England, and perhaps three

hundred thousand, partly aristocratic, in the United States. "The 'Market,' which gave a tone to all English literature, was formed of the aristocracy of England." But at the present time there are probably two million readers in England, "one-half democratic, for democracy has taken long strides over John Bull's acres"; in America there are another two million readers, seven-eighths democratic ("the remainder are the miserable remains of the would-be gentry, allied to the old monarchists, among the ultra whigs").[24] It is not strange that Young America often wrote about "literature for the people" and "poetry for the mass," and that it felt called upon to explain rather self-consciously the function of criticism and otherwise to educate the new audience.

Cheap books and a wide audience had another simple and direct effect on Young America's literary criticism. A reviewer in the *Democratic Review* put it well: "It is a melancholy truth that the business of criticism is in a declining way, like banking; cheap publishing has given it a terrible blow ...." The reviewer explained that when everyone who cared to could buy the book under review, an extended summary of its contents in typical quarterly review style had lost all novelty and interest.[25] Young America's awareness of this fact led to fewer long quotations and more attention to genuine criticism and unfamiliar "good" literature, in its reviews.

The lack of an international copyright law, which contributed materially to the development of mass publishing in the United States, also subjected Young America's criticism to another kind of pressure.[26] Though he and the rest of Young America did not always resist this pressure, Evert A. Duyckinck recognized it fully. The piracy of "cheap and nasty" literature from abroad, he maintained in 1845, led to the puffing of minor American writers simply because they were in competition with cheap foreign literature: "It was felt that American authors were oppressed and driven out of the market by the state of the trade; the strong feeling of nationality in the Press was aroused; and it was determined, however unconsciously, that all the geese that should be produced this side of the Atlantic should be called Swans."[27] More idealistic reasons explain much of Young America's championship of American literature, but the foreign competition is also a factor.

We may notice, finally, a more obvious and "modern" result of the commercialization or democratization of patronage. A book had become a mass-produced commodity, and since the way to sell a commodity to a large market is to advertise, publishers were advertising directly, especially in the newspapers. But they were also using the editorial columns of periodicals for the promotion of books, establishing in this period the familiar point of view of the modern publisher which is described by Randall Jarrell: "From the publisher's point of view criticism is a quite important subspecies of advertising; reviews are free publicity, free testimonials. Good criticism is criticism that sells books. A good critic is a man who likes as much as possible as persuasively as possible."[28]

Having been brought up in his father's bookselling business and having been connected at times with several publishing houses, E. A. Duyckinck was always acute about such matters as this. He pointed out clearly the parallels between literary wares and any other kind of merchandise and between the author and the merchant; and he defended the author and the publisher from the criticism of those who were somewhat horrified at the darkening of the fair name of literature and genius by commercialization: "The most greedy, carnivorous candidate for fame, who bites with the avidity of a pike at a newspaper puff, and urges his literary wares upon the public ... is not half so industrious as the tradesman with his signs, bill-heads, checkbooks, agencies, correspondences, runners, gazetteers, advertisements, with his name on every packing box, placards on every dead wall . . . John Jacob Astor is a man of greater celebrity than his book-keeper, and glorious book-maker on his own account, Halleck. A prolific literary rabbit keeps before the public with some diligence, but not with half the success of the last new pill manufacturer."²⁹ As this suggests, Duyckinck and Young America accepted and used the new methods, and their criticism was naturally influenced.

Duyckinck's work as editor of Wiley & Putnam's series, the Library of Choice Reading, provides the clearest example of the influence. Many of the favorable reviews of the Library as a whole and of individual volumes in the *Democratic Review* and in the *Whig Review* (when Wiley & Putnam was publishing it) were from his pen or directly inspired by his interest: in asking William A. Jones to review the Wiley & Putnam series he pointed out the advantages of a magazine review: "Suppose, instead of these newspaper notices you should occasionally group together a few favorite volumes for a magazine article—for which you could have the additional advantage of being paid." An undated letter of J. T. Headley to Duyckinck is revealing also: "I send a short review . . . of Matthews [*sic*] book. Give my love to Matthews [*sic*] & tell him if there is anything in my article that he could wish cut out he will do me a favor to erase it & I hereby give you *orders* to do it."³⁰ But it should be noticed that Duyckinck was choosing the books to be published also and hence that his own literary judgments were not necessarily violated. Indeed, as we shall soon see, he lost his editorial position with Wiley & Putnam because he would not sacrifice his independence of judgment.

v

The literary criticism of Young America must first be seen, then, as one intellectual manifestation of broad political and economic movements. Young America recognized the new publishing economy and tried realistically to adapt itself to it. It openly and explicitly allied itself with the Movement party of the United States and edited its leading periodical. From the vantage point of this candid commitment and this understanding of the publishing business it could see many literary and critical issues with a clarity denied to many of the conservative critics, whose views were often obscured by their genteel refusal to commit themselves, to admit that they had a vantage point. Whatever may be the faults of special pleading and literary demagoguery that Young America's political loyalties and acceptance of the new literary economy brought to its criticism, these commitments also encouraged it to face the new problems of commercial patronage and a democratic literature and to recognize the merit of the new literature of such men as Emerson, Hawthorne, and Melville.

Instead of wishing, with the conservatives, for the better days of the past, when in literature and politics the leaders were not chosen from below and when "the worst and weakest books" did not "poll the most votes," Young America attempted to educate the reading democracy through its new kind of magazine-review. It rejoiced, as W. A. Jones put it, in the opportunities for the "culture of the imagination" which the poor now had: "people's editions, cheap libraries without end." Not looking backward to the past, but, in the "spirit of the age," forward to further progress, Young America with its faith in political action could hope that a Democratic State would assist publishers and other agents of enlightenment to bring culture to even greater numbers: "The time may not yet have arrived, but it must come some day, when the wealth of the state, joined to the munificent bequests of individuals, will unite to provide classic entertainments; not the mere dole of the Roman people in an early day ... but free lectures, free concerts, free admission to galleries of paintings and sculpture, to libraries, and reading-rooms, to public walks and gardens of rare beauty; and lastly to the 'well-trod stage'..."[31]

CHAPTER II

THE YOUNG AMERICANS

I

THE GROUP of literary critics that came to be known as Young America in the eighteen-forties was a loosely organized literary clique of young men, mainly New Yorkers. The clique grew out of the Tetractys Club, which was formed in the middle 'thirties by Evert A. Duyckinck, William A. Jones, J. B. Auld, and Russell Trevett. Evert's brother, young George Duyckinck, was usually present at the meetings of the club and was later considered a member. Shortly after the four named the club, Cornelius Mathews was brought in; he thanked them for their "willingness to spoil the name of your Society for the purpose of giving me pleasure." Others, including Herman Melville, met with the group from time to time. The quality of its early meetings is suggested by a letter to E. A. Duyckinck, which he read to the club on September 22, 1836; ostensibly from "a party of Young Ladies," it was "fastened on Mathews." The letter addressed these questions to Duyckinck about a society "of which you are said to be a member": Is the name of the society "the Teterass Society," named thus because of "its propensity to put its nose (like that snipe) into muddy waters such as metaphysics, political economy and theology"? "Is it, or is it not true that slings are drunk at its meetings?" What is the source of the noise that issues from the meetings? Do you carry on your conversations in Hebrew? Why does the watch permit your orgies? "Is the following a correct list of its members? Auld—a Locofoco. Jones—a mimic. Matthews [*sic*]—a poetaster. Yourself a ———! Trevett—a zealot. and a military person. One General George?" Do you all have blue eyes and two of you "embryo whiskers"?[1]

---

[1] For notes to chapter ii see pages 133–135.

Undoubtedly many literary projects were discussed at these meetings, whether in Hebrew or not. In a letter to W. A. Jones in early 1839 George Duyckinck mentioned a projected "joint volume," which he hoped would appear the next winter when Tetractys had got together again. This was perhaps *Arcturus,* one of the best "little magazines" of its day (too good to be popular, said Poe), which began publication in December, 1840, under the editorship of Cornelius Mathews and E. A. Duyckinck, and to which the other members contributed.[2]

Later in the 'forties the more or less formal club organization probably lapsed, but the group continued to work together and to share a general point of view. They coöperated on the editing of other magazines like *Yankee Doodle* and the *Literary World.* Relations among them were often strained, especially when the crotchety, ebullient Mathews was concerned; the amiable "Felix Merry," as E. A. Duyckinck signed some of his work, seems to have been the link holding the clique together. Like that New England group, the transcendentalists, to which Young America has some similarity and with which it was usually friendly, the members often united to differ.

II

The members of Tetractys and the later associates of the Young American clique recognized one of their chief prophets and forerunners in William Leggett, the radical intellectual who is best known as an assistant of Bryant on the *Post.* The more politically minded members of Young America looked back to his *Critic* and his *Plaindealer* as a model for some of their periodicals; they admired his style and subscribed to many of his democratic political views. Young American Parke Godwin wrote in the prospectus to his *Pathfinder* that it would follow the model of Leggett's *Plaindealer* and "will sustain what are known as ultra democratic views." Another periodical later continued the form.

Parke Godwin wrote to E. A. Duyckinck, who had probably been the literary editor of the *Pathfinder,* asking him to write for a new weekly, *Young America,* which would be "like the Pathfinder" in design and "democratic in tendency."[3]

Young America as a literary group had many affiliations with the narrowly political Young American movement, more active in the 'fifties, which was publishing these weekly magazines. As we have seen, most of the literary critics shared the radical and liberal political and social views of the Locofocos although, since they were primarily literary men, their chief concern was with the establishment of a democratic national literature.

The more exclusively political and social Young American movement, according to Merle Curti, grew out of the desire of democratic young men in the United States to match the democratic movements abroad—Young Germany, Young Italy, Young Ireland, and the like—with a Young America, dedicated to strengthening the democratic order in the United States and to spreading over the whole world this new and better political order.[4] The weekly *Young America,* for which Parke Godwin wrote and perhaps Duyckinck, represents one activity of this movement. *Young America* had been the *Working Man's Advocate* earlier—a self-explanatory title—and was published by the National Reform Association or Agrarian League, whose chief object is explained in the title of a *Young America* "Extra": "The Jubilee: A Plan for Restoring the Land of New-York or (Incidentally) of Any Other State to the People." *Young America* took its place in New York with other radical journals like *The Subterranean* ("Independent in Everything—Neutral in Nothing"), the *New Era,* successor to the *Man,* and the *Plebian.*

The most energetic and outspoken leader of the political movement later in the 'fifties was George N. Sanders, who bought the *Democratic Review* in 1852.[5] Sanders completely outdistanced all the earlier literary group in his application of political standards to the judgment of literature: his position is almost a caricature of that of the more literary (and more sane) members. But its very exaggeration, in an article called "Fogy Literature," will point up clearly some of the tendencies of the group. Using the books of William A. Jones as a starting point, Sanders launches into a highly rhetorical condemnation of "Fogydom" in literature, "including that old nightmare of American Literature, the *North American Review.*"

The present decrepid [*sic*] health of Fogydom, its attenuated figure, dyspeptic system, shattered nerves, neuralgic stupidity, rheumatic inertness, agueish trepidation, chronic dishonesty, and feverish uncertainty, has been superinduced . . . by the swallowing of such debilitating literary physics . . . English black draughts from an American bottle. Young America does not require such pap . . . It must have fresh, vigorous, wholesome mother's milk, strong as the blood which flowed in '76, not the green tea of parvenu society, nor British concoctions of chalk and water.

American writers who echo English writers,

and *their* crowd of imitators, who exhibit their monthly lunacy in the magazines, with the lesser incubi of your *North American Review,* that superanuated [*sic*] dust-box into which old Fogydom expectorates freely . . . your pale-faced and whiter-neck-tie-universal-desolate-island colonization, starvation-comforting and eternal-torment-nullifying associations' literature . . .

—all "these incubi which sit on American republicanism . . . must be rooted out and deadened."[6]

The earlier group of literary critics did not go so far as Sanders, but their political and social biases were evident to many literary men. Longfellow, in a letter to George W. Greene, dated Cambridge, July 23, 1839, wrote:

The *Loco-focos* are organizing a new politico-literary system. They shout Hosannas to every *loco-foco* authorling, and speak coolly of, if they do not abuse, every other. They puff *Bryant* loud and long; likewise my good friend Hawthorne of "Twice-told Tales"; also a Mr. O'Sullivan, once editor of the "Democratic Review,"—now Secretary of Legation at Paris;—a young man, with weak eyes, and green spectacles, who looks like you, and is a humbug, nevertheless and notwithstanding.[7]

Emerson, who was in many ways a part of Young America's "mutual admiration society" (to use the *Knickerbocker* term for the group), was also somewhat unhappy over the political leanings of some of the group. He told Margaret Fuller that O'Sullivan was "politico-literary and has too close an eye to immediate objects." He sees "Washington" in everything.[8]

III

Against this background of narrowly political Young America and the social and literary Tetractys Club, we may now define in more detail the literary critics known as Young Americans in the late 'thirties and 'forties. In a manuscript summary of his life Cornelius Mathews put forward as one of his claims to distinction that he was the "originator of the 'Young America' Party in the United States."[9] Though he was never modest or quiet in his appraisal of himself or his achievements, Mathews was probably not exaggerating, this time. At any rate he was widely known as the "Corypheus of 'Young America,'" the "centurion of the sect." But despite Mathews's importance and his fame or notoriety, he is of minor significance as a literary critic: he was more active as a creative writer and as a direct propagandist for the passage of an International Copyright Law. Mathews was going to create an American literature himself: *John-Donkey's* satirical description of a "Meeting of the Mutual Admiration Society" at E. A. Duyckinck's home shows his spirit. Present were "Mr. Shadow" (Duyckinck) and "Young America, Esq. (on his behemoth)" (Mathews).

The President, upon taking the chair, remarked that the object of the present meeting was to resuscitate the defunct American Drama, and create a new era in Dramatic Literature. These little jobs would not require, he ventured to suggest, more than half an hour, at farthest—at least, if he interpreted aright the sparkle on the spectacles of his friend YOUNG AMERICA.[10]

And at every opportune or, sometimes, inopportune moment he lectured and wrote on the protection of American literature by law.

Mathews's relation to the Young Americans who confined themselves more closely to criticism is defined in one of E. A. Duyckinck's letters to W. A. Jones. Mathews, who managed to offend all his friends at one time or another, was currently at odds with Jones; Duyckinck, mediating between them, wrote: "Apropos to your article on Poetry for the People [in O'Sullivan's *Democratic Review*], Mathews gets out at the end of the month a vol 'Poems on Man in his various aspects under the American Republic,' quite on the plan you have laid down." He added that he had written an article on them which O'Sullivan had accepted—"subject to some additional alterations of his own." "Mathews of course has read yr article closely and talks constantly of it in the highest terms."[11]

In this letter is revealed the axis on which literary Young America revolved: Mathews, writing poems, plays, novels; Duyckinck and Jones, writing criticism; O'Sullivan, publishing the criticism in the *Democratic Review* with "some additional alterations of his own." As the two most important Young American literary critics, Duyckinck and Jones deserve further attention.

"Mr. Duyckinck is one of the most influential of the New York *litterateurs,* and he has done a great deal for the interests of American letters."[12] So wrote the grateful Poe in 1846, for Evert A. Duyckinck had published Poe's books and given him material encouragment. But Poe's description is accurate: Duyckinck was a *litterateur* above all else, and he had done much for American literature. His father, a prominent New York bookseller, having left him a moderate income, he devoted himself to literature. We need not detail his numerous editing positions on *Arcturus*, the *Democratic Review*, the *Literary World, Yankee Doodle, Holden's Dollar Magazine*, and many others. But we should notice a few of his activities and attitudes that have a direct bearing on his criticism.

Probably the greatest service that Duyckinck rendered American literature was his encouragement of young (and Young) American writers, particularly from 1845 to 1847, when he was the editor of Wiley & Putnam's Library of Choice Reading, a series which grew out of the Home Library, a publishing project which he and William Cullen Bryant had started.¹³ Duyckinck's part in bringing a higher standard of publishing with Wiley & Putnam's Library is described by the *Democratic Review* (at this time not in Young American hands). "At the suggestion of a literary gentleman of this city, who deserves well for his innumerable attempts to serve the cause of letters," Wiley & Putnam began the issue of the Library of Choice Reading in 1845. By March, 1847, the Library had reached its ninety-first volume of American and foreign literature. Referring indirectly (for his name and Young America's are never mentioned) to Duyckinck's partiality to Young America, the *Review* continued: "Now and then it is true, the editor's partialities, or the persuasions of injudicious friends, have led him to incorporate an inferior work into the collection; but as a whole, his labors have been ... highly praiseworthy." The reviewer objected specifically to the inclusion of Poe, Simms, Mathews, Headley, and Cheever, but approved of the volumes of Hawthorne, Mrs. Kirkland, George Henry Calvert, Melville, and Margaret Fuller.¹⁴

In addition to the American writers already mentioned, Duyckinck tried to obtain books from others, some highly respected now. He wrote to Emerson, August 13, 1845, asking him to contribute a book, preferably an entirely new book "written in a popular manner for the best class of readers."[15] Crusty old Richard Henry Dana, who was also asked to contribute, was skeptical about the whole idea of a *series,* seeing in it apparently another example of the "intermeddling with one another," which is "the great curse of that great Curse, Democracy!" He felt strongly about being one of twenty or thirty in a series: "my individuality is too strong in me yet." On the other hand, Duyckinck did decline Thoreau's early *Week,* which Emerson had asked him to consider for the Library.[16]

Many young American authors must have been as sorry as Emerson when they learned in the spring of 1847 that Duyckinck and Wiley & Putnam had quarreled. Emerson wrote to Theodore Parker on May 6, 1847: "I mentioned to you that perhaps Wiley & Putnam would make good publishers—A few days afterwards I was sorry to see that Duyckinck and they appeared to have quarreled,—Duyckinck, with whom I have had some friendly correspondence, & by whom I meant to propose it."[17] The quarrel came over Duyckinck's publishing of works by Young Americans in the series and in the *Literary World,* which he was editing for Wiley & Putnam and Appleton. The *Knickerbocker,* gleefully quoting from its brother conservative, the *North American Review,* a condemnation of the Library for publishing Simms, Poe, and Mathews, explained that the publishers had tried to persuade Mathews to withdraw his book after it had been announced for the series. "The author was offered a cheque for a hundred dollars if he would withdraw it from the series..."[18] Mathews reported on February 20, 1847, that the publisher's "intemperate, indecent, & groundless opposition" to him had caused them to break "clean through their contract with Evert."[19]

Duyckinck's religious, social, political, and literary attitudes were complicated. Apparently he had every reason to fall into the conservative attitude of a man of independent means.[20] And in his religious thinking he tended to follow the orthodox High Church party of the Episcopal Church, to which he belonged. In the Puseyite controversies which rocked the American as well as the British church, he was "something of a partizan in his conservatism among the church champions of the New York Review." But he was too tolerant to side wholly with the party of formalism. His memorialist describes his services in this field:

In this respect he was of great service at a time when culture was in danger of being discouraged by certain church leaders and driven out into nonconforming quarters or secular cliques, whilst stout sticklers for antiquity united a certain grossness of living and habits of self-indulgence with rigid formality and dogged orthodoxy. Duyckinck loved the old English literature that grew up under the combined influence of the University and the Church, and he did much to make the same reconciliation in America, especially in New York and New England...

The tolerance in his religious attitude is strikingly revealed in a diary entry written when he was abroad: "Read the Church service at home this morning after breakfast with Channing's Essay on War."[21]

In political and social affairs Duyckinck's attitude is characterized by a similar tolerance. His tolerant and humane spirit seems to have made him sympathetic toward many reforms and toward many of the policies of the Democratic Party. Young American J. B. Auld, whose Locofoco standards were high ("the Whig party towards which I have a mortal antipathy"), described Duyckinck well: "one reason I like E. A. D. is that he is such a good democrat at heart; although he has a vast degree of toleration."[22] He was at home for years in the columns of the *Democratic Review* and the *Morning News,* which Samuel J. Tilden and John L. O'Sullivan started as a party organ for the campaign of 1844.

But as a relatively "free" intellectual, a professional literary man of sorts, his chief concern was always to promote American literature. That aim, as well as his personal conviction, drew him into the Democratic Party, which seemed to him more promising and sympathetic than the Whig. Of certain young political followers of Whig Horace Greeley, he remarked: "Barren rascals let them suck at the dry dugs of Horace Greeley."[23] His difficulties with editor Francis Bowen, who was trying to wake up the conservative *North American Review,* illustrate this fact also. When Bowen received the article he had asked Duyckinck to write, he thanked him and said that it would need modification on several points: Duyckinck's call for frank political discussions in magazines and condemnation of those magazines that did not permit it would censure the *North American* itself; "you have viewed these little monthly magazines through a magnifying glass, and have exaggerated their interest and importance"; furthermore, "it is as well, perhaps, to confine the eulogy to those who are dead, that we may avoid the appearance of making invidious distinctions among the living." A few days later Bowen returned the manuscript, having given up his attempt to "alter" it to suit his review.[24] As this shows, Duyckinck and other Young Americans were quite willing to publish in Whig or any other magazines when they could; they learned what subjects could be used without offense to the Whigs: Duyckinck wrote W. A. Jones that he would like to see an article on "Religious Poetry" by him "and think the Whig Review would be a more favorable medium for it than the Democratic." In the same letter he told Jones that he had referred O'Sullivan to him for an article on humor and for book notices. Duyckinck helped Jones sell his work even to ladies' magazines: "I have sent MSS to Mrs Kirkland but I understand she objects to bookish critical matter. The fact is pure literary criticism is the last thing needed in the ladies magazines. Serve up narratives—

female biography ...''[25] Duyckinck and Young America found that they could most often "serve up" "pure literary criticism" to Democratic magazines.

Duyckinck's literary outlook shows clearly the two most important literary aspects of the Young America clique. He is notable for his appreciation of rising American authors like his friends Simms, Hawthorne, Emerson, Poe, and Melville. He could appreciate even the more vigorous type of Southwestern humor which found its way into the Young Americans' *Yankee Doodle,* whose motto was "A little more grape, Captain Bragg." W. A. Jones wrote of him: "he is almost rabidly American, as much so as his fastidious and easy nature will allow him to be as a critic—talks of building up our literature, copyright, and the claims of American writers, in the most enthusiastic style compatible with true elegance and a little fastidiousness."[26] And along with this interest Duyckinck and the other Young Americans combined a love for the English writers of the seventeenth century. Duyckinck's enthusiasm was always of a restrained sort, however, and always kept within the bounds of his religious beliefs. When the more bold Melville called Shakespeare divine, and "gentle, aye, almost as Jesus," Duyckinck was shocked and Melville apologized for his irreverence.[27] The terms that W. A. Jones used to describe his essays on seventeenth-century literature are accurate descriptions of all his writings: they contain "graceful sentiment," "easy manner, gracious amenity, delicate fancy, choice taste and subtle humor." It is *descriptive* criticism (rather than *analytic*)." His whole literary character is quite well summed up in Cornelius Mathews's name for him: "Silver Pen."[28]

Yet Duyckinck must not be left on that somewhat negative note. Samuel Osgood spoke of his "conspicuous" part in the "American Renaissance" (Osgood's phrase) and further characterized it, with remarks upon the literary rivalries of the time, as follows.

Duyckinck clung closely to the old English standards of culture, and went stoutly for a New York school of letters that should be a full match at least for the rising New England literature. In that spirit he wrote for the New York Review those fine, thoughtful articles upon George Herbert and men of that stamp, not in a narrow temper indeed, but rather with hearty and generous recognition of the new and startling school that was rising in Boston and Cambridge.[29]

Duyckinck's close friend William A. Jones also played a "conspicuous" part in the "American Renaissance." Well known in his time as a critic and essayist, Jones had a numerous following: in a series of articles on American prose writers in the *Broadway Journal,* he was the first author treated, and the article said that it was a common remark of "good and true men," "skilled in the honest language of nature," that "I always read an article in the magazines that bears the name of William A. Jones." And it was not difficult to find articles by Jones in the New York magazines from 1835 to 1850. Even by 1844, when he was twenty-seven, Jones confessed that he was a little weary of the incessant round of critical essays he was turning out: "For ten years we have dealt pretty extensively in this sort of wares. Literary criticism has been our hobby,—a little over-ridden of late,—and we must confess we begin to tire of the trade."[30] As the quantity (and quality) of his work indicates, Jones was, even more than Duyckinck, a professional literary man. At this period in his life he might truthfully be called a professional literary critic, a rare type in all literary history.

The social and political views of Jones were very much like those of Duyckinck. In 1849 Jones wrote that he believed most of the older members of his family were Whigs, "although all of the present generation who have taken any public stand, or filled office, have been, if we are not mistaken, democratic"; he thought also that his father, a prominent New York judge, though a Churchman and a Federalist, had voted for Jackson.[31]

Jones's own position is clear: his acute analyses of political satire, political poetry, and poetry for the people, in which he stresses the democratic tendencies of past and present writers, are among the most important exhibits of the *Democratic Review*'s "politico-literary system."

His religious affiliations also parallel those of Duyckinck. Of his family in the past he wrote: "The whole family, with very few exceptions, is to be divided into the very opposite ranks of Churchmen and Quakers."[32] Editorial connections with Episcopal journals and his personal letters put him with the "Churchmen," and sometimes with the High Church party on many issues. Yet he was generally tolerant and always maturely intelligent about his religious beliefs. He seldom lets a narrow morality color his critical writing: one of his finest efforts is a vigorous censure of the moralizing children's books of his day.

But all other aspects of Jones's life are swallowed up in his career as a "magazinist"—a magazine critic, a reviewer. He set out to become a master in the critical essay, and on the whole he succeeded. He applied an amazingly wide knowledge of literature to the writing of a new type of review essay: the short, concise, tightly written magazine article, a type of article in sharp contrast both to the heavily learned, verbose essay in the quarterly reviews and to the light, diffuse, superficial, appreciative essay in the more popular monthlies and weeklies. His style is generally in keeping with his purpose: the typical sentence is simple, short, hard-hitting, though on occasion he can indulge in the long, full-bodied periods which were the delight of the more academic rhetoricians of the nineteenth century. His catholic taste and his strong personality result in a style in which many contrasting elements are brought into a tense and live harmony. Into an eighteenth-century prose style he pours critical judgments based on the principles of his master William Hazlitt, leavened with a literary wisdom gained from a close study of minor English writers of the seventeenth century. All in all, Poe's final judgment of Jones is substantially correct (one must say "final," for Poe had earlier called him an *"imitator and a quack"*): in a posthumously published article, Poe wrote: "Our most analytic, if not altogether our best critic, (Mr. Whipple, perhaps, excepted,) is Mr. *William A. Jones...*," adding that Jones's "summary judgments of authors are, in general, discriminative and profound," his papers on Emerson and Macaulay "pointed, lucid, and just." Whipple, said Poe, is superior as a critic of poetry, but he has "less discrimination" and "a more obtuse sense of the critical office" than Jones.[33]

Rufus Wilmot Griswold may be correct in attributing Poe's later approval of Jones to personal friendship—the mutual admiration of the Young American clique. But his judgment is a good summary of Jones's qualities. Jones was a literary man and a critic primarily, an analytic critic at his best in the criticism of prose, and especially in the analysis and criticism of "sentiments" (ideas, moral and intellectual attitudes). He was weak at, and in fact despised and rarely attempted, the old-fashioned verbal criticism of the Scotch rhetoricians—and Poe.

Two other Young Americans, John L. O'Sullivan and Parke Godwin, came into the group from outside Tetractys, and since their interests were not primarily literary their activities need not be detailed. O'Sullivan was correctly called in 1845 "a scholar, an ambitious politician, and something of a revolutionist."[34] Aside from his editorship of the *Democratic Review,* O'Sullivan's chief claim to historical note is highly appropriate to a Young American. Julius W. Pratt has almost definitely established his coinage of the term "Manifest Destiny."[35] O'Sullivan's expansive, eloquent, sanguine personality seems to have led directly to his belief in the manifest destiny of America, and to the success of his editorship of the *Democratic.* Julian Hawthorne described him as "always full of grand and world-embracing schemes" and added that "it was difficult to resist the contagion of his eloquent infatuation." Among the successful resisters were such differing people as Longfellow, who called him a humbug, and Poe, who once called him an ass; but, significantly, transcendentalist Thoreau called him "one of the not-bad" and Democrat Hawthorne looked upon him as "a dear friend of mine."[36]

Another "politico-literary" Young American, Parke Godwin, son-in-law of William Cullen Bryant, was more closely associated with the *Evening Post* than with the *Democratic Review*. He was identified in the 'thirties and 'forties with such radical and rather impractical idealistic forces in the country as Fourierism. After 1850 he continued to be a spokesman for political Young America.[37] His literary criticism is consistent with his social idealism; one of his most notable articles is one on Shelley.

Many of the writers and critics often called Young Americans by their contemporaries are of no direct concern to us here. Some contribute to the *Democratic* only occasionally; others, not at all. Samuel D. Langtree, co-editor of the *Democratic* until his death in the early 'forties, contributed criticism to the early numbers of the *Review*. John Inman, so far as I can learn, did not contribute to the *Democratic*. Joel T. Headley and John Bigelow made many contributions to the critical cause of the Young Americans and were close friends of the central members of the group. Margaret Fuller, C. F. Briggs, George P. Morris, and other minor writers were occasionally close to the group. One editor on the fringe of Young America, Charles Eames, may be cited because he provoked a description that might apply to most of the group. The *Aristidean* said that Eames, then editor of the *New World,* was "a transcendentalist, yet not all transcendental," reminding one "a little of Coleridge, a little of Brownson, a little of Carlyle, and a great deal of Emerson." "He is a 'friend of progress'..."[38]

Other, more famous writers were in one way or another and at particular times closely associated with the group. William Gilmore Simms, though in Charleston most of the time, had close social relations with the group when he was in New York and corresponded voluminously with them. Politically he shared some of their reforming zeal; in 1846 he wrote to E. A. Duyckinck that he would like to send one or more poems a month to O'Sullivan for ten dollars a month: "I propose to make a Series of Sonnets ag. the punishment for death & in reply to Wordsworth, & to deal otherwise with practical subjects in the same manner. Say this to O'S."[39] He worked with as much energy as any of them to promote a distinctively American literature, as may be seen in his published critical essays and his unpublished letters. He wrote to Duyckinck that the authors of America "may do wonders yet," if they only work together; the first step must be "to disabuse the public mind of the influence of English and Yankee authorities," who have "fastened our faith to the very writers, who, least of all others, possess a native character," such writers as Longfellow and Irving. The opponents of Young America often classed Mathews and Simms together for violent critical disapproval, and Simms returned the criticism in kind, though he gave up more quickly than did Mathews: having given the editor of the *Knickerbocker* the lie in print and cut him in public, he let Duyckinck and Mathews continue the fight, being "loth [*sic*] to soil my fingers with the skunk."[40]

Lowell in his younger, more liberal days was sympathetically inclined toward the group but repelled by the enthusiasm and excess of Mathews. Lowell is called a Young American in 1843 by E. A. Duyckinck in his diary; his attitude toward Mathews is shown in a letter of the same year to Duyckinck: he asked to be remembered "affectionately to Jones and the rest," but at the same time laughed at Mathews: "I laughed when I saw the advertisement of M's serial works with the effervescence about 'Young America.' "[41] Five years later in the *Fable for Critics* Lowell was still smiling at Mathews. We shall notice later his radical contributions to the *Democratic Review*.

At a later date Melville took his place in the group, socially and intellectually. On a famous outing in the Berkshires, Melville, Holmes, Mathews, Duyckinck, Hawthorne, J. T. Headley, and others had climbed Monument Mountain, "rambling, scrambling, climbing, rhyming—puns flying off in every direction, like sparks among the bushes," and had returned to a three-hour dinner "from turkey to ice cream, well moistened by the way." Holmes, one report continued, "drew the whole company out by laying down various propositions of the superiority of the Englishmen. Melville attacked him vigorously. Hawthorne looked on . . ." Melville rather than Mathews, it will be noticed, rose to the bait, for he was particularly violent in his Young American spirit at this time. In Duyckinck's *Literary World* he was calling for new American writers and for new critics to back them against Europe.[42]

Other writers were sometimes close to the group. Poe (especially when Duyckinck was publishing his books and when Young America was approving his attacks on Longfellow), Bryant (whose Democratic Party allegiance made him acceptable), Hawthorne, and Emerson were all at times identified with the group and benefited from their critical approval. Longfellow, Irving, Cooper, the elder Dana, Halleck, and other representatives of an older rather stagnant culture were almost never identified in any way with Young America.

IV

The influence of the group is shown clearly in the reaction of their enemies. The opposition in New York centered around the Whig journals the *New York Review,* the *Whig Review,* and the *Knickerbocker*. Such critics and editors as George Hooker Colton, Edward William Johnson, Lewis Gaylord Clark, George Washington Peck, Edwin Percy Whipple, Henry Norman Hudson, Rufus Wilmot Griswold, Charles Wilkins Webber, and Henry Hope Reed opposed their political and literary views.

If George N. Sanders represents the extreme to which Young American doctrines could be carried, perhaps Fitz-Greene Halleck and the elder Richard Henry Dana represent the extreme on the other side. Bayard Taylor described Halleck as an anachronism, an alien in a modern world: "neither republican, democratic in the ordinary sense, Protestant, nor modern," "he was congenitally monarchical, feudal, knightly, Catholic, and mediaeval." Halleck flatly stated that "as a Federalist in my boyhood and a monarchist in my manhood, I prefer a government representing property." His literary views are indicated in a friendly argument with Young American Jones over the merits of Pope and Fletcher—Halleck, of course, contending for the superior rank of Pope, Jones, for Fletcher. That Dana shared Halleck's political and some of his literary views is attested in many places. In a letter to W. A. Jones, Dana reported an incident at a dinner with Bryant: Dana and Halleck talked of the virtues of a monarchy and a nobility; Bryant was shocked when they declared that they were serious. Dana commented drily: "Bryant still holds to simple democracy, I believe." In personal letters to Duyckinck, Dana argued many times against Young American positions: an American literature could not be forced into being; nothing good could come from Democratic "theories, schemes, associations." He was glad in some ways that Duyckinck's *Literary World* had ceased publication in 1854: Duyckinck could turn to something better than weekly articles "&, pray God, not adulterated with any of your Very-American-ism"; "you are a modest man personally—why cannot you be so nationally?"[48]

Other enemies were not so polite nor, often, so extreme in their conservatism, but they fought Young America in the press and not in personal letters. The combination of political and literary motives in the opposition is best seen in many articles in the *Whig Review,* some of which will be referred to in later chapters. Here we may notice two influential enemies whose writings suggest the impact of the clique on American literary life.

Lewis Gaylord Clark, editor of the *Knickerbocker,* used his magazine for many attacks on the group, centering his attention on Cornelius Mathews and William Gilmore Simms. In December, 1845, the magazine told its readers about the "new dynasty":

as there may be some among our readers who do not know that a new dynasty has been established in the American Republic of Letters, for their enlightenment in part, and in part to justify ourselves from the serious charge of uttering slanderous words against the Corypheus [Mathews] of "Young America," we must needs waste a leaf or two of our Magazine, which might certainly be filled with better matter.

No reader of the *Knickerbocker* could remain ignorant of this dynasty very long: Clark flayed them in nearly every issue. He missed no opportunity, rejoicing, for example, when the *Literary World* passed out of Young American hands temporarily in 1847: the *World* "will now be well conducted"; "it will become the organ of no clique, nor the disguised puffer of well-established humbugeousness or unsaleable literary wares."⁴⁴

Perhaps no one criticized the clique so frequently as did Clark, but many others found occasion to laugh or sneer at them. The conservative Whig anthologist Rufus Wilmot Griswold conducted a long battle with them, which culminated in the Duyckincks's publication of an encyclopedia of American literature to supplant his earlier anthologies. An early skirmish found Griswold going out of his way to snipe at Young America in his *Prose Writers of America.* He wrote his friend James T. Fields that he dreaded the appearance of the book: " 'Young

America' will be rabid." Ridiculing the whole group in the anthology, he wrote, among other things:

Our "Young America" had not wit enough to coin for itself a name, but must parody one used in England; and in its pronunciamento in favour of a fresh and vigorous literature, it adopts a quaint phraseology, that so far from having been born here, or even naturalized, was never known among us, except to the readers of very old books and the Address of the Copyright Club.

Young America responded as Griswold had predicted; Griswold lamented:

Inman, Parke Godwin, W. A. Jones (how *could* Whipple puff that miserable diluter of old New Monthly articles?)—E. A. Duyckinck, J. B. Auld, and the whole mob of "Young Americans," (pish!) "swear terribly" that they're omitted, and the amiable Cornelius, centurion of the sect, is so "abused."

Duyckinck, who had hopefully prepared a sketch of Mathews and made a selection of his works for Griswold's book, was particularly wrathful when he discovered that his praise had not been used. Instead of using the puff of the book that Griswold had sent him for use in the *Literary World,* he prepared his own biting review. Almost ten years later Griswold avenged himself by a similar review of the Duyckincks's new *Cyclopaedia of American Literature.*[45]

v

Having seen something of the origin of Young America, the critics and authors associated with the group, and their enemies, we may observe finally that these liberal Democratic literary critics represent a new group of the intelligentsia in American life, the professional literary critics. It is a striking fact that all the leaders of the group—Duyckinck, Jones, O'Sullivan, Mathews, and Godwin—had studied law. As Lowell's *Fable* put it:

Thus a lawyer's apprentice, just out of his teens,
Will do for the Jeffrey of six magazines.

But these apprentices did not go on to practice law; they became professional literary men.

W. A. Jones, a professional critic, illustrates the importance of this fact in an article called "Amateur Authors and Small Critics." Jones began by dividing all authors and critics into two groups: the professionals and the amateurs. It would be absurd, he said, to call upon an amateur lawyer or physician with the expectation of competent treatment of one's difficulties. "Few do that well 'for love' which can be better done for money." If in ordinary concerns it is true that the "laborer is worthy of his hire," it is much truer "when we ascend in the scale of labor, and come finally to that which most tasks the intellect and requires the greatest number of choice thoughts."

In literature, no less than in law and medicine, the best work will almost always be done by the professional, who "puts his heart or invests the whole stock of his faculties" in his pursuit. The professional critic will not be one of those who are the "most opinionated of all critics," "the people of sense in ordinary matters, and men intelligent in their own walk of life, but who have never received any tincture of literature."

Jones's very scorn of the amateur critics, the "small critics," shows how much the professional spirit had developed by the middle of the nineteenth century.

Correctness is the height of his ambition. He remarks how many lines in a poem end with a monosyllable, or with a similar termination. He pretends to be skilful in metres, and the art of poetry. By this he intends the rules of Aristotle, and Bossu, and Blair, and not the divine instincts of the glorious Afflatus... The small critic is delighted with petty beauties and the minutest details. He loves still more to carp on petty faults in a great man... Originality puts him out; boldness he styles extravagance, and acknowledges none but imitative excellence. All inventors, he looks upon as arrogant interlopers. He is distrustful of novelty, and apprehends failure in every new scheme. He cannot distinguish between freshness of feeling and affectation. He has a horror of individuality, and will not allow the weight of personal impressions ... He is a newspaper Thomas Aquinas, or the Duns Scotus of a monthly."[60]

The professional periodical critic had arisen to analyze, interpret, and judge the productions of the new group of professional authors who were also just achieving a place in American society.

Chapter III

YOUNG AMERICA'S THEORY
OF CRITICISM

I

To UNDERSTAND Young America's criticism, we must consider the group's theories and assumptions about the function and method of literary criticism, as well as Young America's social milieu. The adoption of a critical or aesthetic theory or of a particular method of criticism may have only an indirect influence on the practice of criticism. As R. P. Blackmur says of all critics, "the personal element in a given critic—what he happens to know and happens to be able to understand—is strong or obstinate enough to reach into his aesthetic theories"; few critics have a coherent philosophy; "aesthetics sometimes seems only as implicit in the practice of criticism as the atomic physics is present in sunlight when you feel it."[1] Young America's theories of the critical function and of the mode of criticism that the critic should employ were approaches or roads into the literature of the time. Or they were assumptions underlying the group's critical practice. The theories are not so influential as to make predictable the critical results, but they are significant in determining the course of the criticism.

And the subject has a somewhat more intrinsic importance, too. The theory of criticism has a place of its own in the history of ideas. The Young Americans writing for the *Democratic Review* made a contribution, however slight, to the history of the ideas on the purpose and method of criticism. For the same reason, it is of some importance to see what attitudes and methods they put into practical use.

---

[1] For notes to chapter iii see pages 135–136.

In the simplified and arbitrary classifications that follow, I have attempted to allow for the difficulties of classifying critics or critical attitudes and modes. No good critic, not even a Locofoco Young American, can be classified; no good critical essay follows a single, uncomplicated mode of criticism. Yet some attitude and some method may predominate: we may say with Edmund Burke that "though no man can draw a stroke between the confines of day and night, yet darkness and light are upon the whole tolerably distinguishable." We can distinguish certain attitudes and methods which are found in the criticism of Young America and its contemporaries.

The critics of this period, particularly the Young Americans, fortunately make the task of distinguishing the kinds of criticism less difficult. They often felt called upon to speculate upon the nature of criticism, to make remarkably explicit their critical methods. The newness of the professional literary critic in American life, the democratization of literature, and the attempt of the magazine-review to appeal to a wider public—all called for some explanation of the proper activity of the critic to the relatively untrained reader.

There was, moreover, a widespread opinion, reiterated in article after article, that the nineteenth century had been and was primarily a critical age: W. A. Jones even apologized for restating a truism: "It is too late in the day to talk after the fashion of scientific discovery, of the critical character of the age." He expressed the conclusion that many critics drew from this belief when he said that in an avowedly analytical age, "in which criticism has flourished almost to rankness, it seems necessary to criticise occasionally the critics themselves, in order to learn where to fix our faith, whom to trust, and how far to credit any one of them."[2] The resulting criticism of criticism permits us to see Young America's theory of criticism explicitly stated in many articles.

The significance of Young America's choice of a critical attitude can be gauged only after we notice briefly the prevailing theory and practice of all the critics of its time. What were the critical attitudes and methods of the time? Four attitudes toward the function of a critic are "tolerably distinguishable": the critic should be judicial, or prescriptive, or interpretive, or impressionistic. The methods or modes of criticism may be separated into two general methods: formal, "Neo-classical," Aristotelian criticism and ideological, "Romantic," Platonic criticism.[3]

II

At one extreme were those critics who retained the attitude most common before 1835: the critic was a judge before whom a literary work appeared. The judicial critic, possessed of a code of laws or "rules," decided "This will do" or "This will never do." In its narrowest form, the judicial attitude led to dogmatic, arbitrary, unsympathetic judgment of art according to unanalyzed personal standards, or according to more objective standards derived from the observation of ancient models or from the "laws" of human nature. The standards could be narrowly moral and result in violent emotional reactions. The judicial attitude was a conservative attitude which could find little to approve in modern writing simply because it was different from older writing. Similar to and often going along with the extreme judicial attitude was the prescriptive attitude which directed advice and even offered stylistic changes to the author before the bar. Typically the judicial and prescriptive attitudes were found in the critics who followed formal modes of criticism.

At the opposite extreme from the judicial, dogmatic critic was the impressionistic critic, who attempted to make, properly speaking, no judgment upon the literary work before him. In its loosest, most diffuse, and relaxed form impressionistic criticism recorded merely the random adventures of a soul in literature. The impressionistic critic exclaimed upon beauties and publicly "appreciated" literature. He was of what Margaret Fuller called "the gentle affirmative school" of critics. He told his highly personal reactions to a literary work, and though he had underlying critical assumptions which governed his impressions, he did not consciously attempt to work by them or to make them explicit.[4] The impressionistic critic necessarily followed the "Romantic" method in his criticism.

Between the two extremes one finds those critics who felt that the critic's job was primarily one of interpretation. The interpretive critic thought that his function was to explain, to make himself a bridge between the author and the public, or to guide the public through the intricacies of an unfamiliar work of genius. In the middle nineteenth century the interpretive critic often compared himself to the priest who mediates for the people; one writer, who veered toward the judicial attitude, carried the analogy further and spoke of the critic as a literary Pope, who may grant absolution for authorial sins. The interpretive critic typically followed "Romantic" methods of criticism.

Young America seldom took the judicial attitude in its criticism; it did, indeed, judge literature, but it did not submit literature to various tests and, after a cold and rational analysis, judge its merit according to its degree of adherence to established rules, as did such judicial critics as Blair and Kames, who were strong influences on American criticism before 1835.[5] Young America, in fact, spoke strongly against judicial criticism. E. A. Duyckinck called Lord Kames "a dogmatic critic," refuted one of his "bilious assertions," and remarked that his *Elements of Criticism* was now a "poor authority with scholars." The "small critics," several times scornfully described by W. A. Jones, are judicial critics, who, skillful in the "art of poetry," by which they mean "the rules of Aristotle, and Bossu, and Blair," affect "the dictatorship of letters."[6]

Somewhat more often Young America fell into the prescriptive attitude, assuming that it was writing as much for the author as for the reading public. The tone was usually fatherly and came most often from those Young Americans who had most experience as editors, an occupation that accustomed them to giving advice. Young America's awareness of the democratization that had overtaken literature also led to the prescriptive attitude: many of the new young writers who were flooding the market with volumes of their "effusions" undoubtedly needed advice. O'Sullivan commented when he was reviewing Griswold's *Poets and Poetry of America* on the astonishing quantity of "very decent verse which is poured forth by every day's fresh issue of its fresh periodicals of all sorts"; large quantities could be collected each year, "all rising up just so high and no higher—all intolerably tolerable." But as a Young American he could not wholly disapprove, since the large number of American poets was one of the results of the spreading of "a certain degree of education" and of the "influence of republican institutions" which suggest "that sentiment of *equality* which scorns to shrink from what other men, named Milton, or Shakespeare, or Byron, or Shelley, or Wordsworth, or Bryant, have attempted and achieved."[7]

But he could give advice to them such as that to young George Hooker Colton, later editor of the *Whig Review*. The "fatal facility," he wrote, of Colton's measure, his exuberance, his copiousness of language have led him in *Tecumseh* to attempt too much. He should have spent more time and written less, but "we desire" to encourage Mr. Colton and would not want him to think us too severe: "Mr. Colton has the Poet in him" and can make the world admit it.

Let him persevere. Let him labor—write, re-write, condense, polish, and above all freely blot and burn. Let him forget Scott, if he can, and sign a total abstinence pledge against the octosyllabic. Let him *think* for himself ... Let him choose, moreover, themes in truer harmony with the genius of his age ... The trump of martial glory has long lost the power it once possessed to rouse and thrill our spirits with its splendid rage, and the true poetry of the age has virtually cast it aside ... Let Mr. Colton choose a better theme ... and write in a spirit more akin to the young progressive and aspiring spirit of his time, ... let him write with a deeper concentration of thought and labor within less limits of space and larger limits of time,—and we are greatly mistaken in his present tokens of promise, if he is not destined yet to take a high place in the Pantheon of the literature of his country.

Or, in shorter form, let him be a liberal Democrat instead of a conservative Whig and write well and he will be a great poet.[8]

But neither the prescriptive nor the judicial attitude was Young America's dominant attitude. Along with most other critics in that "critical age" they had found a new attitude, and, however much in practice they might revert to the dogmatic criticism of an earlier day, their theories of the critical function always called for interpretive, sympathetic criticism of some kind.

One of the clearest statements of the Young American position appeared in the first volume of the *Democratic Review*. A favorable review of Emerson's *Nature* (probably by O'Sullivan or Langtree) identified the critic with the priest. The greatest writers, the greatest minds, are far above the reach of ordinary, conventional minds:

As, however, they do not think and speak for their own order only, as they desire to address and receive a response from the great majority of minds—even from those that doubt their own power of going into the holy of holies of thought for themselves—there is needed the office of an intermediate class of minds, which are the natural critics of the human race. For criticism, in its worthiest meaning, is not, as is too often supposed, fault-finding, but interpretation of the oracles of genius. Critics are the priests of literature.

And another writer on Emerson in the sixteenth volume said much the same thing, as he quoted: " 'the office of criticism is to bridge over the waters that separate the prophet from the people—to compass the distance that divides the understanding in the auditor from the intuition of the utterer.' "⁹

The critical attitude of Young America and the *Democratic Review* is further demonstrated in its approval of Margaret Fuller as a critic, but W. A. Jones's description of the true critic, which is very much like that of Margaret Fuller, summarizes well enough their belief.

The true position of the genuine critic [said Jones] is not yet acquired. In the republic of letters, he sits just below the poet. Wanting his invention, with less imagination, less fancy, he is still his equal in honest enthusiasm; in independence, perhaps superior; in a love of the beautiful, only lower, because he has less poetic power; in a reverence for the good and true, a faithful brother; of an accurate perception, clear judgment, and yet a lively sensibility, all working in an atmosphere of the purest candor and liberality, the critic is the advocate of the poet, the exponent of the feelings of the people towards him, the middle-man between the two.

The critic has a high duty to perform: "Pure literary criticism, no less than a high moral standard of right, must exert a most salutary influence upon the public mind." We must look, consequently, for "a more enlightened and liberal school of criticism than has yet subsisted here." America, as "the freest of modern states," especially needs good criticism "to preserve liberty from degenerating into licentiousness, and democracy from falling into popular disorder."¹⁰

In keeping with their serious reforming spirit, Young America and the *Democratic Review* seldom indulged in impressionistic criticism. Even such an inveterate personal reactor and appreciator as Henry T. Tuckerman tried to be philosophical and less exclamatory when he was writing for the *Democratic Review*.

III

When the critic has defined his function, he must discharge that function according to some critical method or mode. However much violence it does to the complexity of each of the many methods of criticism, two polar extremities in critical method may be set up (two monstrous entities which have never really existed). At one extremity are those methods of criticism which have been labeled scientific, technical, formal, "Neo-classical" (or "Classical"). The historical line of critics who follow these methods may be traced back through such critics as Dr. Johnson, Du Bos, Bossu, Dryden, Boileau, Ronsard, Puttenham, Scaliger, Vida, and Horace, to Aristotle. These methods analyze the formal characteristics of literature as an "art," an "imitation." They are devoted to technical studies of poetic diction, of the structure of the epic and other genres, of tropes and meters and stanza forms. The critics practicing these methods are generally of a group in society—an intelligentsia or an aristocracy—which is little concerned with changing a social and economic order that has been good enough to give them the leisure in which they may study "art" carefully.

At the other pole are those means of ordering critical analysis which are variously called ideological, dialectical, poetic, scholarly, sociological, historical, psychological, "Romantic," and Platonic. These methods, in one form or another, are to be seen in the Marxist and Neo-humanist critics of recent times, in Arnold, Ruskin, Taine, Hazlitt, Coleridge, and finally, in Plotinus, Longinus, and Plato. They are concerned with analyzing the "ideas" (or if more strictly Platonic "the Idea of the Beautiful") in literature, which is an imitation of *life*. Similarly the methods may concern themselves with genetic studies of the social (or "historical") and psychological background out of which a literature grows. Typically, literary critics who follow these methods are likely to be more—or less—than literary critics: like Arnold and the Marxists they often become primarily social critics concerned with changing society. Others become philosophers, historians, psychologists, or, coming full circle, artists (using one work of literature as a basis for another work of literature).[11]

Where Young America stood on this matter may be seen first in a quarrel with Edgar Allan Poe, in the course of which these polar extremities clash clearly and directly. In the "Exordium" to the review section of *Graham's* in 1842 Poe quoted from Cornelius Mathews's preface to the first volume of *Arcturus*. Mathews, representing the ideological critic and Young America, said that criticism in the nineteenth century has a wider scope than in the past. It turns over errors in grammar, imperfect rhymes, and false quantities to the proofreader; "it looks now to the heart of the subject and the author's design. It is a test of opinion." Criticism is philosophical, liberal, and generous.

A criticism, now, includes every form of literature, except perhaps the imaginative and the strictly dramatic. It is an essay, a sermon, an oration, a chapter in history, a philosophical speculation, a prose-poem, an art-novel, a dialogue; it admits of humor, pathos, the personal feelings of autobiography, the broadest views of statesmanship.

To this the formal critic, in the person of Poe, answered: "We respect the talent of Mr. Mathews, but must dissent from nearly all that he here says." Criticism in the nineteenth century can be no different from criticism in any other time. The criticism of the modern Germans and other true critics differs not at all in principle from the criticism "of Kames, of Johnson, and of Blair," who understood the unvarying "laws of man's heart and intellect."[12] The art of criticism cannot neglect its duty of pointing out errors in grammar, rhyme, and quantity. And to say that it must be "a test of opinion" is to be so vague as to be meaningless.

Criticism is *not,* we think, an essay, nor a sermon, nor an oration, nor a chapter in history, nor a philosophical speculation, nor a prose-poem, nor an art novel, nor a dialogue. In fact, it *can be* nothing in the world but—a criticism.

Of that "conglomerate science" which is "anything and every-thing at once," "we know nothing, and really wish to know less." But it should not be given the name "criticism." *Arcturus* and Young America should find another word. Have they "any objection to Orphicism, or Dialism, or Emersonism, or any other pregnant compound indicative of confusion worse con-founded"?[13]

Their Whig enemies found other names for Young America's method of criticism. According to one *Whig Review* critic, the "transcendental-Boswell," "Concord or sub-Goethean," eulogis-tic, "aesthetic method of criticism" has resulted in little but "extravagant sentimental eulogies"; "even now we are expecting the publication of a promised eulogy, by a certain democratic editor, on the name and hellward career of Maximilian Robes-pierre; the frightfulest idol whom God ever sent upon men for their sins."[14]

Whatever the method might be called, Young America, not only through Cornelius Mathews in *Arcturus* but also through many writers in the *Democratic Review,* made its belief in ideo-logical criticism explicit, and it ventured certain political and social reasons as well as literary and philosophical for its belief. Critics in the progressive nineteenth century should be concerned with ideas, opinions, and the like:

Critics, poetasters, and *quasi* literati, prattle of style as of a thing of first consequence, and will with profound gravity, deliberately con-demn the most masterly conceptions, because the style is not monot-onous like Gibbon, or as faultlessly inane as the Spectator. The taste of the age is now changed, and shrewd men discover that to be pos-sessed of ideas is the first requisite; the next, to express them as clearly and correctly as possible.

Another critic put the "mechanical critics" among the aristocracy who objected to democratic principles. "Despite the canons of an envious criticism, which has mistaken the machinery for the product of the mechanism, we hesitate not" to say that the true inspiration of poetry comes from "universal philanthropy." "All poetry, indeed, is essentially democratic."[15]

Among Young Americans the outstanding theorist about critical method was not the extravagant Mathews but W. A. Jones. Jones consciously refused to construct a complete, philosophically reliable critical system. He distrusted the narrowness of all philosophical sytems: their reasoning, he said, is inconclusive, the evidence likely to be unsatisfactory or insufficient. The most important result of philosophical speculation is the "sharpening of the critical faculties." But an adherence to one system will breed intolerance. On many of the most important philosophical problems "the proper state of mind appears to be that of philosophic doubt," which will promote clearness and a tolerant temper. For "systems are invariably one-sided and exclusive, exhibiting in general but a partial view of any question ..." "Truth lies between the extremes of opposite theories."[16]

Jones was acquainted with most of the philosophical theories of criticism from Plato and Aristotle down to those of his own day, and the method that he used for a particular essay was varied to suit the literary work under discussion. But in one way or another the emphasis was upon "Romantic," ideological criticism in theory and practice. Negatively, he often expressed his dislike of merely technical criticism, of the hard, scientific formality of Aristotle and the Scotch common-sense philosophers.[17] And more positively, his critical master was William Hazlitt— "the first of the regular critics in this nineteenth century, surpassed by several in some one particular quality or acquisition, but superior to them all, in general force, originality and independence."[18]

But Jones, in good Young American fashion, seems to have learned his critical method from an American as well as an English and European tradition. Without sharing R. H. Dana's political views, Jones (and Duyckinck) recognized his critical pioneering in introducing a "new conception of criticism" to America, the method of Schlegel, Coleridge, and Hazlitt. On almost every point Jones's critical attitude and method represent a culmination and an extension of Dana's ideas. The opinion of Hazlitt is typical: Dana, according to William Charvat, "was almost alone in his appreciation of Hazlitt's prose style," in the years before 1835; Jones, however, has gone farther; he objects that Dana is "unnecessarily harsh on Hazlitt."[19]

Jones's critical method and his recognition and tolerance of many types of criticism are best seen in two essays in the *Democratic* in 1844, "Critics and Criticism of the Nineteenth Century" and "Criticism in America." Beginning with a historical survey of English criticism, he described the "old, conventional, Anglo-Gallic principles of taste and opinions" brought into England at the Restoration. In the reigns of William III and Queen Anne this taste was confirmed, and it led to the perverted code of taste and philosophy of aesthetics which could see nothing good in Elizabethan and Jacobean literature. The age must be credited with having produced great comedy, periodical writing, satire, "manly and sensible political writing and preaching." But it was deficient in "imagination, philosophy and the higher kinds of genius." The criticism, like the original writing, "was just but tame, its prudence degenerated into mere caution, it was timid, nay almost servile." The "perfect embodiment" of the period was Dr. Blair, "a sensible guide on the less abstruse questions of criticism and taste," "a clear, methodical teacher of Rhetoric," and "intrinsically ... no contemptible writer." With the establishment of the *Edinburgh Review* a change came in the prevailing mode of criticism; it brought a "new style of criticism, fresh, original, independent," and generally fair (with well-known exceptions).

With this "new style of criticism" in mind Jones is able to answer the question, How are good critics to be known and distinguished?

By these several signs; a thorough knowledge of the subjects, periods, characters, books, upon which they write; a mastery of the genuine spirit of the age—its needs, its aims, its faults, its tendencies; by a good, if not elevated, standard of criticism—(some topics and classes of writing do not require a lofty standard); by generous justice, by genuine feeling, not mawkishness nor sentimentality, but sincere feeling—for a critic should have a heart as well as a head, a fact too often overlooked or forgotten; by a knowledge of rules, but no lack of the fit spirit to guide in the use or adaptation of them; by experience and skill in the art of writing.

The critical method reflected here is obviously one which would place great emphasis upon the sociological background, upon ideas, and upon sympathetic understanding of the author.

And the good American critic must come up to further exacting standards:

Much general acquirement, knowledge of life and character, dabbling in science and the arts, thorough knowledge of history, and (at least) American politics and economy, with good sense and good feeling, honesty, tact, taste, judgment, and a style, clear, readable and attractive—these are necessary for all.

And a first-class editor and critic must have something more: "distinguished logical powers, a pure tone of elevated popular eloquence, and that delightful turn for pleasantry that enlivens a paper, as a cheerful disposition enlivens life itself." It will be noticed that the method reflected here was one that Poe, the technical critic, could not approve of, for his critic, as such, would have no use for history, politics, economy, and general science.[20]

Other shades and types of "Romantic," ideological criticism were fully represented in the critical practice of Young America in the *Democratic Review*. But predominant among the types was always the critical method which seeks out the ideas in literature, especially the democratic ideas in literature, the mode which leads finally, according to Whig E. P. Whipple, "to the conclusion that Joel Barlow was a greater man than Homer, because he entertained more liberal notions of government."[21]

IV

Young America was, then, almost never strictly judicial in tone, somewhat more often prescriptive; it believed that the critic's function was interpretation. Wholly apart from the more strictly intellectual "spirit of the age," the rise of the professional critic had much to do with making the interpretive spirit dominant. The critic felt his importance.

The dominant methods of criticism in Young America's theoretical discussions and in their practice were those which concerned themselves with an analysis of the "content" and the "background" of literary works. The "spirit of the age," that watchword of the Movement party, demanded that criticism be "a test of opinion," that the critic concern himself with the mind of the author, with historical setting, with the "spirit" and "organic form" of literature. And, of course, Young America preferred the "new" opinions and ideas which were in harmony with the progressive, democratic, American spirit.

Finally, we must be reminded of the caution with which we began: no good critic can be classified; no good critical essay follows a single, uncomplicated mode of criticism. Indeed, one is tempted to generalize that the success of criticism is directly proportionate to its lack of systematic adherence to one attitude and method of criticism. The generalization expresses at least a significant half-truth about Young Americans: the best critics were those who said with W. A. Jones that "truth lies between the extremes of opposite theories." The best critics seem to have been those who resisted the excesses of the dominant "Romanticism" perhaps in a manner characterized as typically British by Walter Jackson Bate. We might substitute *American* for *British* and *English* in his description:

The manner in which leading English critics of the early nineteenth century avoided the excesses of both emotionalism and subjectivism is mainly attributable to a more than usually active presence in this period of qualities which are distinctively British: to the empirical but compromising good-sense which traditionally characterizes British thought at its happiest, and to a stubborn refusal to accept for long any systematization.[22]

However they were able to avoid them, the less systematic Young American critics, at any rate, were less likely to fall into the characteristic vices of each attitude and method: they could more easily avoid the narrowness typical of the purely judicial, prescriptive, technical critics or the easy judgment, the complacent literary democracy, and the irrelevancy typical of the purely interpretive, impressionistic, ideological critics.

Chapter IV

YOUNG AMERICA'S THEORY
OF LITERATURE

I

Having noted the influences on Young American critics which were exerted by their social milieu and their beliefs about the function and method of criticism, we may turn to a consideration of the content of the criticism—what the critics had to say about literature itself and about specific writers and schools of writers.

The first matter of importance in considering the content of the criticism—and the concern of this chapter—is to discover the answers to certain fundamental questions: What is literature? What is poetry? and fiction? and the essay?[1] What is the function and purpose of literature? What is good literature? What is the relative importance of the various forms of literature? The first part of the account which follows will summarize the theories and generalizations with which Young America attempted to answer these questions.

Of major significance also in criticism are the recurrent themes with which many critics concern themselves. The last part of this chapter will turn to two themes which seem to be of most importance in this period: literary nationalism, and morality in literature.

II

The Young Americans and most of the other critics of the time seldom discussed *literature* theoretically; that is, they used the term *poetry*, the highest and most typical kind of literature, in discussing literary theory. When we see Young America's definition of *poetry* we see, by and large, its definition of *literature*.

[1] For notes to chapter iv see pages 136–139.

The Young Americans' basic principles of poetry are not at all distinctive; with most other critics of their time they assumed the validity of a familiar "Romantic" theory of poetry. They shifted the approach to poetry from the text of the poem to the "maker" or "creator" of the poem. Poetry, great literature, and indeed the fine arts of whatever form, they maintained, are created by the *genius* whose *higher* faculties (those which are the farthest removed from the senses and which work in the realm of ideas) are fully developed. The realm of ideas in which the genius finds the spirit with which his works are animated is the same realm in which the ideas and spirit of religion dwell. There is little essential difference between the beautiful and the good and true.

The poet's *imagination,* they continued, enables him to soar into the higher regions of spirit and idea and to make *actual* to his readers the *real* which he sees there. A closely related attribute of the poet is *taste,* which "consists essentially in a perception of the beautiful" in the actual world. Furthermore, the true poet of genius reveals in his work a "profound insight into our moral nature"; he attains an inner self-knowledge of common human nature. The poet is disposed to believe in religion and the reality of the spiritual life associated with it; he loves beauty for itself as the religious man should love virtue.[2]

The conservative opponents of Young America generally held these beliefs also, but in the *New York Review,* the *Whig Review,* and other conservative magazines they did not emphasize the same aspects of the fundamental principles as did Young America: they attended to the higher reaches of the philosophical theory (especially in the *New York Review*), paid close attention to the process by which the poet symbolized the ideas with which he was concerned, saw the true poet combining thought and image into an organic unity; conservative politically, religiously, and socially, they tended to emphasize the

conservative ideas which must be found in poetry: the idea symbolized, to state it bluntly, had better be traditional and orthodox,
and preferably highly moral and religious.

Starting from the same point as their opponents, Young
Americans did not follow the conservatives upward into philosophy or backward into religious orthodoxy or to the right
into moral and political conservatism; they moved ahead and to
the left. Democratic Young America emphasized that side of
"Romanticism" which was interested in the common man and
reform: the ideas that the American poet's imagination found
in that higher realm should carry the names Democracy, Equality, Freedom, and Brotherhood. And to "Romanticism" it added
a less abstract and vague set of doctrines which may be characterized as Utilitarianism, though the doctrines may not be strictly
Utilitarian and their origins are certainly not to be found exclusively in the philosophy of Bentham and his followers.[3]

Yet, however weak or strong the direct influence of Utilitarianism, the prevailing tone of the answer of Young America
in the *Democratic Review* to the question, What is Poetry? and
the attitude toward all imaginative literature is much like that
described by George L. Nesbitt as typical of the "Benthamite
Reviewing" in the *Westminster Review*. The *Democratic,* like
the *Westminster,* had a "positive ideal for literature, a New
Literature to fit the New Man in the New Age." The two periodicals made similar charges against much traditional literature:
it was useless in practical affairs, often, as Plato said, false and
misleading, and controlled by the aristocracy ("fiddling while
England starves"). They both wanted a "new and useful literature" which was not merely decorative. We may parallel Nesbitt's summary of another aspect of the *Westminster*'s attitude
with a similar statement by a Young American in the *Democratic.* The *Westminster* felt that "the intelligent philanthropist
first devises means of improving bad physical conditions. He

does not spend his life reading poetry to the indigent ..." W. A. Jones wrote:

The infusion of popular feeling into our works of speculation, the great aims of reforming, enlightening, and, in a word, educating the people and impressing the importance of the individual,—this is one of the great problems of the age, and perhaps *the* Problem. To render man physically comfortable, and to give him sufficient occupation, of whatever sort circumstances demand, is the primary duty of society; but, immediately next to that, to seek to elevate and refine, deepen and expand, the characters of all men ...

And, as we shall see, many are the opinions in the *Democratic* that would echo the *Westminster Review*'s statement, quoted by Nesbitt, "It would be a pity that poetry should be an exception to the great law of progression that obtains in human affairs; and it is not."[4]

Two articles, among many others in the *Democratic Review,* may be cited to show that there was a direct influence of Utilitarianism upon the thought of the *Democratic* reviewers and that it was used to oppose Coleridge's conservative "Romanticism." An article on "Jeremy Bentham" opened thus:

A writer in the Westminster Review [J. S. Mill, in August, 1838] remarks, that the two men of the present age, who have most strongly influenced the minds of their countrymen, are Samuel Taylor Coleridge and Jeremy Bentham. Without questioning the accuracy of the observation, as it respects Coleridge, we think there can be no doubt of the truth of so much of it as applies to Bentham. Whatever may have been the influence of the former, whose researches were mostly in the region of abstract thought, and whose sympathies were altogether with the past, it must have been of that occult and delicate nature which only a few learn to appreciate. But the influence of Bentham, with his rugged sense, with his contemptuous disregard of authority, with his bold onsets upon cherished modes of faith, and with the immediate interest attached to all his inquiries, must have made itself felt speedily, and that in a shape which might be easily recognized.

The article proceeds to summarize some of the important ideas of Bentham and to recommend them to the young men of the nation at this time when they "are attaching themselves to sentiments of democratic freedom and progress." And again, in "Mill's Logic," the *Democratic* reviewed favorably the school of thought which found expression in the *Westminster Review*. The reviewer hoped that John Stuart Mill's contributions to the *Westminster Review* would be collected and published as Macaulay's essays had been. He held Mill's *System of Logic* to be a "noble production," "which will distinguish the age."[5]

But, no matter how great was the direct influence of Utilitarianism on the thought of the Young American critics in the *Democratic,* the criticism was still based upon the Romantic premises. Such typical *Democratic* critics as E. A. Duyckinck and W. A. Jones also wrote a few articles for the conservative *New York Review* and the *Whig Review,* and their answers to the question, What is Poetry? were not out of harmony with the answers made by other critics in those journals. Their answers used the familiar terms *imagination* and *genius*. They could both go so far as to stress the religious element in poetry, with which the *New York Review* was particularly concerned, and the *Whig* also, but somewhat less obsessively. In the *New York Review* Duyckinck could argue "not that all poetry must be religious— but that the best poetry, and worthiest the name, that which enters into the nature of man, his passions, and affections, which represents his character must be essentially so."[6] W. A. Jones could assert in the *Whig Review* that "the imagination should . . . be cultivated, if only as an aid to the strengthening of virtuous resolves and the heightning [*sic*] of religious aspiration," for "the highest poetry, we repeat, is religious." He added later: "It must be confessed, then, the imagination is the most religious of our faculties, and consequently the grandest."[7]

As each continued the development of his ideas about poetry, however, we see the change in emphasis that made these critics find their real place in the reforming atmosphere of the *Democratic*. Duyckinck in the *New York Review* placed Crabbe "with all true poets" because he is moral and religious. But Crabbe, he added, has another important distinction: he was the first to break "the chain of studied refinements" in pastoral poetry; he turned poetry to fresh, new soil.

Long before the Lake school appeared, he had taught the world poetry might descend to the philosophy of common life, might enter into the sympathies and hopes of man, might be familiar with his most ordinary emotions without losing the least of its lofty energy. He was the first poet of the poor. He first carried the light of poetry into the rude cabin of the villager, and recorded the humble history of poverty.

It is pleasing to remark, Duyckinck continued, that this age is recognizing the worth of Wordsworth and Crabbe and is realizing that "the relations of life, however simple, afford the true ground of poetry." The age is made better by such works as the *Lyrical Ballads* and *The Borough;* "question not their claim to poetry." He maintained that a denial of their claim is founded upon a misunderstanding of the nature of poetry; poetry is born of the "simple and pathetic" as well as the "lofty and the imaginative." The spirit of poetry, he concluded, is not to be limited in its application.

Its fresh source is in the human heart; its province is in the wide map of human relations; it is bounded only by the horizon of human emotion; its heritage is the race of man,—and its task-work is to connect and blend the sentiment of the true, the good, the beautiful, the infinite and eternal, with all the passions and emotions that beat in the heart of universal humanity.[8]

In similar fashion Jones continued his development of the fundamental beliefs. In *Arcturus* he went on to rejoice in the opportunities for the "culture of the imagination" which the poor now have: "people's editions, cheap libraries without end." He looked for further progress, to the day when the state and private benefactors would put culture within the reach of all. And it is not only for the sake of religion that the imagination should be cultivated. A "general diffusion" of the "culture of the imagination" would bring many results in earthly society. Among other results are these:

The heart of man ... would be truer, and more affectionate; more earnest, and more confiding. Man would converse with his fellow man as with a brother and a friend ... The natural warfare of trade, the competition of business, would be merged in an universal harmony and brotherly love. The cordial grasp of the hand ... would not be simulated for foreign purposes. The body social would then be in its most perfect state; for "out of the heart cometh all the issues of life;" and then the heart would be the ruling principle of the world.⁹

The spiritual ideal in poetry and other works of the imagination is not a conservative ideal in these accounts; it is progressive and in harmony with the "spirit of the age." We shall see how this variation on the basic theme is elaborated as we trace Young America's movement toward the left in the *Democratic Review*.

As we have seen earlier, the *Democratic* was established partly to encourage the development of a distinctively American and democratic literature. Much of what it had to say on the subject in its early volumes can best be seen later when we examine Young America's pleas for a national literature, for the early statements do not go far toward developing a theory of poetry or literature. The first article, the "Introduction," probably by O'Sullivan, called for the development of a new literature which would be filled with the "animating spirit" of our democracy. One purpose of the magazine would be to vindicate "the true glory and greatness of the democratic principle by infusing it into our literature." But O'Sullivan and Langtree did little more than shout their demands rather shrilly and review such American writing as seemed to contain a new spirit. In the first volume, for example, they praised highly the unorthodox truths in Emerson's "Nature—A Prose Poem"; Emerson and other "minds of the highest order of genius," who draw their truths "most immediately from the Supreme Mind," "have a natural tendency to withdraw from the *conventions* of their own day."[10]

A few months later, Democrat Edwin Forrest's Fourth of July oration (probably written by William Leggett) gave them an opportunity to discuss somewhat more fully the qualities of great literature and true poetry. The opponents of democracy in the United States, the reviewer declared, were formerly able to boast—justifiably—of having within their ranks " 'all the religion, all the wealth, and all the learning' " of the country. Today the "spirit of true religion," at any rate, is allied with democracy; but the "claim of the anti-democratic party to the wealth of the country, will not be disputed." "All-powerful" wealth has, however, not been able "to draw the literature of the country wholly into its sordid grasp."

Mind, immortal mind, disdaining the association, has clung to those holy democratic principles, which allow it the exercise of its highest, noblest qualities. The success of democracy is the greatest conquest that mind ever achieved over matter, through the agency of man . . .

It is, indeed, one of the glories of literature in whatever form genius has cast it "that it has ever been the advocate of those broad principles of human liberty and of that independence of thought which have been the aim and object of the democratic movement in all ages of the world." While the political history of England is a history of the suppression of the common man, its greatest literature reflects the high character of its people untainted by monarchy. The great truths of political philosophy which the United States has had the "happy destiny" to reduce to practice will be found throughout English literature, "cheering the heart of the seeker in the magic of its immortal eloquence, and in the happiest inspiration of its heaven-drawn song." The reviewer continued as follows.

All poetry, indeed, is essentially democratic. Despite the canons of an envious criticism . . . we hesitate not to make the assertion that the truest inspiration of the muse has been drawn from that pure fount of universal philanthropy which invigorates with perpetual greenness the eternal principles of freedom. Poetry can never be made the instrument of oppression, and the poetry of England, in particular, has gloriously contributed to swell the mighty current of democratic feeling which is now spreading over the world, and which promises results so vast for the future destiny of the human race. We speak of *literature* in its highest and most restricted sense.

The reviewer closed by conceding to the opponents the claim to the wealth of the country, but for democracy he claimed the learning and the genius of the country. "What name is there, that conspicuously adorns American literature in all its departments, that cannot be found on the catalogue of the democracy . . . ?"[11]

Other early articles add little to the general theory. Parke Godwin in reviewing Bryant was pleased to discover that the holy instinct of democracy guided him, that his subjects, imagery, and spirit were American. O'Sullivan repeated his introductory plea for an *American* literature in his article "The Great Nation of Futurity." A reviewer of American poetry discovered that our poetry "has felt the influence of that spirit of progress which seems to have marked everything pertaining to this new world"; as social and political conditions have improved, the noble arts of literature have also; our authors have created strong bonds of "common feeling" which help tie the nation together.[12]

After the *Democratic Review* transferred its editorial office from Washington to New York in 1841, the quality of the literary criticism improved. O'Sullivan, Langtree, and Godwin were always more interested in politics and society than in literature. What Emerson said of O'Sullivan applies also to the other two: we have noticed earlier that he wrote Margaret Fuller early in 1843 that "the man is politico-literary and has too close an eye to immediate objects," adding that *"Washington* is supposed in every line of the 'Demo. Review.' "[13] But if Emerson had observed the course of the *Democratic Review* more closely he would have noticed that it was becoming more literary, that, as he wrote, the more literary of the Young Americans were beginning to develop in it a theory of literature that did not look exclusively to immediate objects. Young America and the *Democratic* never attained the aloofness of Emerson, what W. A. Jones called his "certain 'precision' stateliness of manner," his "mortified look of a Puritan," the qualities that mark him as "a sort of male sibyl"; the *Democratic* always declared itself rather noisily on the political issues of the day and felt a "deep sadness in seeing a man of genius [Emerson] thus cold and lonely," "a cool spectator of greater struggles than the world ever saw before."[14] But Young America looked at literature perhaps as closely as did Emerson, whose eye wandered too, even if in another direction sometimes.

Young America began the serious development of its peculiar contribution to a theory of poetry and literature quite logically with two articles cast in general terms. "Democracy and Literature" starts from the general principle that "the spirit of Literature and the spirit of Democracy are one." The author and the scholar are the greatest patriots and contribute the most to the national honor. And, too, "the natural sympathy with his race, that innate love of his fellow creatures which every manly heart delights to cherish, more than anything else contributes to impel the author to stand forward as the advocate of humanity, the friend of the oppressed, the defender of the rights of man." The reviewer then turned to demonstrate that the "moralist, the historian, and the poet, the three intellectual characters who include all others, are essentially democratic." The conclusion with respect to moralists may be summarized: "Pure ethics is *democracy moralized,* to speak after the quaint fashion of our forefathers." Of historians we may say that "the thorough historical student," as, for example, Bancroft, "must become a believer in democracy." And of poets—"The remark is often heard that poets should never become politicians, because politics is a business, and a severe study besides, not a pure 'business of delight;' and yet we find the greatest poets have uniformly been the warmest partizans ... We learn, too, that, despite of the airy charms of romance and the splendor of glittering gauds, the true poet is inherently and almost necessarily a republican." We may look for instances to Milton, Dante, Marvell, the early Coleridge, Southey, and Wordsworth (before they "apostatized from their early creed"), Leigh Hunt, Lamartine, Burns, Béranger, Körner, Schiller, and Bryant. (Shakespeare was not mentioned: he gave the *Democratic Review* trouble; Milton was more satisfactory and was often called the greatest English poet.)[15]

A month later a review of Thomas Campbell's *Life of Petrarch* provided an excuse for further general comment.[16] The usual questions assert themselves: "What is good verse? What makes a good or a great poet?" These questions the critic will answer in the "tone of our age and country," in the skeptical spirit "which tries the spirits, and likes to see things proved."

For, the reviewer continued, there is proof even in poetry: it is intrinsically good or bad. Unless the mind producing it is "instinct with immortality," it is merely form without substance— a result, in Campbell's phrase, of "'tactics in the march of words.'" Certainly "the age has a soul, and the true poet has his mission to speak to it," to speak to all hearers "who are true children of the age; all who, while the long sleep is not yet fallen on them, would fain be up and doing,—aye, up and doing good; and something great, if possible—but let it be good first." This is the true spirit of the age, which Longfellow catches in his immortal poem: "Life is real, life is earnest ..." Progress has left behind the trumpet and warhorse as subjects for emotion.

And for the ordinary citizen who understands this spirit of the age, "what is Poetry?" It may be hard to say precisely what poetry will please him, but certain qualities it must have:

He who will have minds march to his music should have some progress in his own; he should cheer us on, and go before like a trumpeter, not sit like a fiddler ... and keep us promenading up and down; and yet most poets do so. They seclude themselves ... and go round and round in one circle of ideas; and, so far from to-morrow finding them farther than to-day, in any progress towards knowledge, it is a chance rather if yesterday did not. The age marches and leaves them behind, as it must all non-practical men.

The true poet should learn about the world, mix in the bustle of affairs, observe and feel the collisions of practical interests. Such a poet will not write much, but what he writes will be full of meaning, a "reflection of his life," a guide to those who come after. He will contribute a grain toward "the building up of human perfectibility."

Poets of the past, the reviewer concluded, have misled us by glorifying "amatory nonsense," the "joys of intemperance," the "honors of tyranny and cruelty." They have failed to see poetry in the affairs of the common man in private life. "The mute Milton must be reproached that he is also inglorious ...,"[17] Today we must have something different. "The step humanity is now taking, the object it is now seeking, the inspiration which is now breathing through the vast mind of the million, must somewhere reach its sublimest conception, and find its loftiest and purest expression, and *there* is the Poet of the Age." If his theme be deep, broad, and general, he will be the poet of all ages.[18]

As the conservative "Romantics" would have agreed, it is the animating spirit of poetry, not the form, that is important. But this critic was not thinking of the same spirit as the conservatives, who, in the journals across the political fence, were maintaining the essentially conservative nature of all genius. A. Cleveland

Coxe in the *New York Review* had called for a religious poetry for "this country, where we reverence nothing for antiquity's sake," a poetry which, "once well diffused among the people, would have the happiest conservative influence." Theories like these of Young America were for H. N. Hudson in the *Whig Review* a "peculiar, half-ridiculous, half-terrible madness sprung from the marriage of a spurious democracy and a bastard transcendentalism." E. W. Johnson in a *Whig* article aptly titled "The Progress and Disorganization" even denied the validity of the whole concept of the "spirit of the age." The phrase, he maintained, is "a large, a loose, and a captivating one," but it is a "fallacious and sounding" generality. It is but one more sign of the general decline and disorganization into which, in the name of Progress, have fallen all modern literature, religion, and politics. He stated flatly that as yet in America "there are not causes, external to literature, which acting upon it, can, unless very slowly, displace that which we inherit and give us a new one." C. W. Webber called upon American writers to learn from Hawthorne ("if it be the fact that he is ranked among the Loco-Focos, it is the result of sheer accident") that "Higher Conservatism upon the eternal base of which all wise and true Whigs have planted their feet." He added that "if Jonathan had only listened to 'Conservatism,' of whatever kind—either political or literary—" he would not have found himself in such a "snarl" as he is in today with only "Defalcation—Repudiation—Bankruptcy—and the writings of a certain great 'Original Translator,'" to show for all his "'go ahead' hurry to consummate 'Ultimate Destiny,' 'Free Trade,' and 'a Hard money Currency.'" Despite what "their Loco Foco majesties would say to such impertinence," the *Whig Review* would "keep quietly on in preaching" conservatism.[19]

From the sounding generalities of the first two articles Young America did "go ahead" to show how the democratic spirit of the age had been anticipated in earlier literature, was now expressing itself in new poetry for the people, and would in the future manifest itself in a "great Poet of the People," a "world-renowned bard," a "Homer of the mass." Helped occasionally by Parke Godwin, E. A. Duyckinck, John L. O'Sullivan, and a few others, W. A. Jones contributed most of the later variations on the Locofoco literary theme.

The chronology of the articles makes it quite likely that Jones wrote the general article on "Democracy and Literature," which appeared in August, 1842; at any rate, in September, 1842, he began a series of papers on political writers with "Political Theorists of the English Commonwealth"—Milton, Marvell, Harrington, Algernon Sidney, and Andrew Fletcher. He followed this in October with "Political Pamphleteering"—L'Estrange to the present—and in December with "Political Satire and Satirists"—Dryden to the present. When he reached Wordsworth in his catalogue "of the most eminent Poets who have been deeply occupied in politics," he paused to theorize and to discuss Wordsworth more thoroughly.

In "Wordsworth's Sonnets to Liberty," he began by asserting that "in its most comprehensive sense, we might call all poetry political: for all truly inspired verse is the outpouring of the Spirit of Freedom, and the Spirit of Humanity." A similar spirit animates the poet and the patriot. Under the reign of despots, music, declamation, and other arts can flourish, but true poetry and eloquence wither. "All the master-bards, and the vast majority of lesser lights (so they burn with original lustre), of necessity are eulogists of freedom in the abstract, as of the Law of Right, the Law of Truth, and the reverence of the Beautiful; for, without these, what were poetry but a mere heap of fables and false devices." We may conclude that poets are "the most moral, the most metaphysical, and we may add, the most political" of all writers.

As the "right popular philosopher" the poet must propagate "free principles and liberal ideas," even if "only on the shallow grounds of diplomatic expediency." Poets are by their vocations "humanitarians" and "philanthropists," and "feel as no other race or class of men can feel": "the whole circle of human necessities, from the lowest animal desires, up to the most elevated spiritual impulses, is included in their sympathies; and, those, too, of the most delicate and intelligent description. The Poet is the brother of his fellow-men and 'Creation's heir,' with the same fortunes and a similar destiny." From this point Jones descended upon Wordsworth, whom he saw as a great poet but nevertheless an aristocrat: "neither in theory or practice ... does the mass occupy his whole mind." He promised for the next and last paper of the series a description of "a new and very important department of Poetry"—a form of the "Divine Art" which is "most closely connected with the movement spirit of the age— Poetry for the People."[20]

But the next paper had the disconcerting title "Royal Authors" and was virtually the first in a new series of three articles; at the end of the first Jones wrote: "From Royal we shall descend to Noble authors; and, coming down at last to commoners of genius, finally reach the reign of pure Democracy, the only atmosphere in which the plant of genius may expand and grow." Certain wise qualifications of the democratic theory of poetry are found in the first two articles.

In a passage that reminds one of Jefferson's democratic belief in a natural aristocracy, Jones and the *Democratic Review* declared their belief in one kind of aristocracy, the "nobility of Nature," "God Almighty's Nobility." "Democratic as we are, we yet contend right loyally and reverently, for the sovereignty of mind, the aristocracy of genius, the high rank and precedence of talent." Kings of the intellect may be found even in America. "The Republic of Letters has been singularly so named. It is to be feared that, like a Patriot King, it is a mere chimera." But no other aristocracy may be allowed, for the "mere rich man may not be of it, nor the haughty noble," nor, "least of all, the royal claimant, as the exhibition of power is too apt to diminish as you exceed the scale of fictitious rank." There might be "even here in these democratic United States of America, an institution, in name at least, resembling the Royal Academy of Artists." Entrance into this Royal Society of Authors "should be considered a badge of honor and an assurance of governmental protection."[21]

When Jones finally arrived at "Poetry for the People" he began with a short description of the "predominant fact" in the history of the nineteenth century: the rise of the people. This "peculiar feature in the character of the age" has led to a new application of poetry to life "which may be expressed in the phrase, Poetry for the People." We must understand something more about the nature of poetry and its relation to life to see the significance of this fact.

Poetry always conveys the truest and most striking features in the countenance of the time. The most accurate painters of men cannot fail so to portray their master passions, reacting upon contemporary opinions and current modes of thought and action, but that he must needs also depict the contemporary influences by which these, too, are moulded; and these influences combine what we popularly describe as the Spirit of the Age. The patriarchal period, the splendid hierarchies of the ancient and modern world, chivalry ... all point to peculiar tendencies in the times wherein they flourished. The present epoch of literature and popular sentiment must have its mouth-piece also, and this it finds in Poetry for the People.

Jones described the qualities that the true poet of the people must have and the subjects he must treat—"the necessity and dignity of labor," the "native nobility of an honest and brave heart," the uselessness of "conventional distinctions of rank and wealth," the cultivation of liberality and generosity, an "honorable poverty and a contented spirit," and "the brotherhood and equality of man." He then reviewed the poets of the people, such poets as Burns, Schiller, Elliott, Crabbe ("a Poet of, but not strictly *for,* the People"), Miller, Clare, Prince, and Shelley. He concluded by expressing the belief that this department of poetry will be the great department of American poetry. He looked forward to the coming of the "Homer of the mass": "With a pen informed by experience, and exercised on the immortal themes of the poet and the philanthropist, with hope in his heart and love on his tongue, with the fire, the fervor, the frankness of genius, such we would gladly hail, the Poet of the People and the Poet of the Poor."[22]

Young America's Locofoco poetic theory appeared in later articles, but there are no significant theoretical additions. And still other articles carry poetic theory in somewhat different directions. A transcendental ally of Young America, Orestes A. Brownson, was discussing aesthetics in the same issues that displayed Jones's theories. In the number in which Jones described poetry for the people, Emerson described a "high poetry," which would be "wholly new, the latest birth of time, the last observation which the incarnate Spirit has taken of its work." But Walter Whitman, not yet Walt Whitman, the "Homer of the mass," had nothing to say on poetic theory at this time; his contributions to the *Democratic* were sentimental stories of the people. We have earlier noticed, however, that he was later to pay tribute to the intellectual stimulation provided by the *Democratic* in this period. And Whittier, suggested by Jones as one who might become the great Poet for the People, was attempting in his "Songs of Labor" a few months after Jones's article to *be* a people's poet in the *Democratic.* The young James Russell Lowell in such contributions to the *Democratic* as the poem on Prometheus, whom he called "the first reformer and locofoco in Greek Mythology," had ambitions in the same direction: "no poet in this age," he said, "can write much that is good unless he give himself up to this tendency [radicalism]." Even William Gilmore Simms, as we have seen, hoped to contribute radical poems to the magazine, and other less familiar names, like Rh. S. S. Andros, were making attempts in the *Democratic* to write a democratic poetry for the people.[23]

III

For several reasons an account of Young America's theory of fiction may be brief. As I have said above, to the critics of this age the term *poetry* usually stood for all literature, including fiction (especially when a novel or short story seemed of surpassing merit). A genius was a genius, no matter what *form* his creations took, and his imagination operated in much the same way in poetry, fiction, painting, or whatever. Consequently, when one has seen the theory of poetry one has seen much of the theory of fiction: the critics were seldom categorical and Aristotelian in their separation of kinds. The highest compliment a critic could pay a novelist or tale-writer was to call him a poet. Said W. A. Jones, "Hawthorne is a true poet..."[24] Thus, when a critic wished to theorize about literary art, he usually theorized about poetry.

But again the chief contribution of Young America and the *Democratic Review* to a theory of fiction is not to be found in their adherence to beliefs held generally at the time. Perhaps the most distinctive principle of Young America was merely an application, to the novel and the tale, of its principle that poetry should show the progressive democratic spirit of the age. What has made Dickens and his work popular? "The chief secret of his extraordinary success is to be found in the accordance of the spirit generally pervading his writings with the democratic genius now everywhere rapidly developing itself as the principle of that new civilization, whose dawn is just brightening upon the world." The reception accorded Dickens in this country is a sign of the appreciation of the only true greatness: "the greatness of goodness, and of genius faithfully applied to its high mission of the improvement and elevation of mankind." He takes his readers among the masses; he shakes aristocratic pretensions and will "hasten on the great crisis of the English Revolution (speed the hour!)."[25]

Growing out of this interest is a more significant contribution to criticism: Young America pointed out, as did Poe, the importance of the tale as a literary form, being especially interested in those stories which dealt with fresh, new subjects of American life. Duyckinck's critical views had practical results, for as editor of Wiley & Putnam he published many volumes of tales, thus providing subjects for review by himself and Jones. Duyckinck wrote a laudatory essay on Hawthorne's tales (Number 1 in Wiley & Putnam's American Library was edited by Hawthorne; Numbers 17 and 18 were Hawthorne's *Mosses*); he published Poe and probably wrote the critical article in the *Whig;* he published Mathews and wrote about him for almost every periodical; an unknown critic praised highly the tales of Heinrich Zschokke (published by Wiley & Putnam); Jones found much to admire in the tales of the South and the West (published by Wiley & Putnam).

But again W. A. Jones's discussion best summarizes Young America's point of view. Jones believed that shorter works of literature of all kinds were of great importance in the present day, and were to be of greater importance in the future. "We have few histories, and long poems (thank heaven!) but abundance of critiques of all kinds, political, literary, theological and characteristic essays, on all subjects, of manners, morals, medicine and mercantile policy; sketches of life and scenery; letters, from abroad and at home, tales, short biographies and every possible variety of the lesser orders of poetry." And as for the future:

We apprehend that literature of this grade and character—short, to the point, interesting—will be the prevailing literature for a long time to come. The chief instruction of the people, their main intellectual resource of amusement, also, will be found in the periodical press. In a busy age of the world, the mass of men (even of readers) have little leisure. This they cannot and will not devote to long, abstract treatises on religion or politics. Our middle age epoch may not come for ten centuries; meanwhile we need to read much and rapidly.[26]

In "Tales of the South and West" Jones amplified his views on the tale. English critics, Jones began, have noticed "the facility of invention and power, with skill of execution, of our writers of fiction." The article on American fiction in the *Foreign and Colonial Quarterly* praises American fiction justly, but it does not mention some of our best writers: Dana, Mathews, Poe, and Simms. One of the places the American genius can best be seen is in the short tale. Without considering the works of Irving, Hawthorne, Dana, Brown, and Cooper, "we still can point to a large body of writers of fiction, tales, 'miniature novels,' (which Schlegel thought the best form of the novel,) and narrative sketches, affording convincing proof, if any could be wanting, that imagination, at least adequate to the production of a prose fiction of the first class, and creative power, are not wanting here, and which, employed on American themes, whether of history, character or manners, legend or landscape, cannot fail to give our literature a national character, which, indeed it is every day acquiring." Besides the "genuine originals" (Irving, Dana, Hawthorne, Brown, Cooper, and Poe) there is a long list of competent "tale-tellers": Miss Leslie, Miss Sedgwick, Mrs. Kirkland, Mrs. Farnham, Judge Hall, John Neal, Joseph Neal, Briggs, Hoffman, Mathews, Sands, Bryant, and Leggett. Jones would agree with the English critic

that though more unpretending in form than the regular novel, the skill of tale writers, with their best attempts, "contains more characteristic excellence than is to be found in the library of accredited novels." We have no one admirable novel except perhaps the Pilot; all Cooper's fictions, admirable as they are in scenes and particular descriptions, being confessedly, even according to Mr. Simms, Cooper's heartiest critic, excellent only in those passages, and abounding in faults elsewhere. But we do possess, without dispute, a body of expert story-tellers, to be cherished and made much of, and to be (a serious climax) STEREOTYPED.[27]

A final important contribution of Young America to a critical theory of fiction was its attempt to define humor and its recognition of the importance of humor and its realism as a characteristically American kind of literature. The humorous works of cantankerous Cornelius Mathews set off most of the discussion and even provoked intramural quarrels in the Young American school of writers.

E. A. Duyckinck contributed the best theoretical discussion of humor as an introduction to a review of Mathews in the *New York Review*. Since the theoretical positions are only implied in the *Democratic,* we may turn to this article. Young America wanted an American humorist as much as it wanted an American Poet of the People. Duyckinck called upon American humorists to "separate the true qualities of a man from the common-places that surround him, and illustrate life by the contrast between a soul such as nature made it, and society in its thousand abuses reflects it." They should look at humanity not satirically but lovingly in order to find "traits of divinity even in the infirmities of our nature," for "this is the high end of comedy," which does not merely make us laugh but gives us hope and encouragement. Duyckinck maintained, in opposition to the "bilious assertion" of Lord Kames, that the humorist is worthy of the highest esteem. "The prince was honest in his lament over poor John Falstaff, 'I could have better spared a better man.'"

Humor, for Duyckinck, had close relations to poetry: its humanity causes it to leave behind the ludicrous as it becomes pathetic; carried a few steps farther, "the incongruities of farce have reached the refinements and inventions of poetry." In the surprise and unexpected contrasts that cause the illiterate to laugh there are "already elements of the serious to the reflective." Humor and poetry are both unlike the commonplace; both attempt " 'to accommodate the shows of the world to the desires of the mind.' " "So we look upon a humorous writer as a kind of familiar domestic poet." "Audrey asks of Touchstone, *is poetry a true thing?* Humor is true and honest in the same sense; and one proof of this is, that it [unlike wit] does not flourish on the artificial level of high life. Humor is not elevated like poetry in its difference from the common sense of things; still, it is diverse, and often represents a better state of feeling."[28]

Starting from comments in William Gilmore Simms's review of Mathews, W. A. Jones discussed "American Humor," a controversial article in the *Democratic* that provoked Poe's wrath and resulted in quarrels among the Young Americans, much to the delight of their enemies. Simms had maintained that America had no humor, that Americans and Englishmen were not a humorous people, that published American humor (except for Judge Longstreet's work) was a blank. Jones exclaimed, "Shades of Irving and Paulding, and Sands and Holmes, assist us! Quips and cranks and wit pellets of Prentice, Lumsden, Jenks, Sol Smith, Neal, and all ye newspaper wits, pierce and puncture ... this awful heretic ..." To refute Simms's assertion that like the English we are too serious, earnest, and devoted to practical pursuits to "feel free to make sport and fun," Jones pointed out that the English are the best humorists in the world: Dickens and Smollett alone have more humor in them than all the French, German, and Italian novelists put together. And in America: "The sources of American humor are various and novel, the scheming Yankee, the wild Kentuckian, the generous Virginian, the aristocratic Carolina Planters [attention Mr. Simms], the Camp meeting, the negro music, the auctioneers and orators, and fashionable clergy, life on the Mississippi and the Lakes, the history of every man's life, his shifts and expedients, and change of pursuits, newspaper controversies, fashion in dress, militia trainings, public lectures, newspaper advertisements, placards, signs, names of children, man worship, razorstrop men." In good Young American fashion Jones pleaded for more national humorists like the national painters such as Mount. His survey of the humorous essayists, fiction writers, and poets mentioned Franklin, Wirt, Irving and Paulding, Hawthorne, "John Waters," "Felix Merry" (E. A. Duyckinck), Sands, Hawes, "Harry Franco," Miss Leslie, Mrs. Clavers, and Cornelius Mathews (more a wit than a humorist, according to Jones). He concluded by pointing especially to humorous advertisements as a rich and "original field of American humor." "The land of patent medicines and candies, and all sorts of curious wants."[29]

IV

The tendency of the hierarchy of forms to break down in this period led again, as with fiction, to the consideration of the essay in its best form as essentially a type of poetry.[30] The great essayists, sermon and lecture writers, and orators were "Prose-Poets" or simply "Poets," who happened not to have put their writings in verse form. But W. A. Jones, probably the best critic of prose in the period, did treat the essay and its related, more utilitarian forms as a separate kind with its own peculiar qualities. In almost twenty articles in the *Democratic,* and many more elsewhere, Jones discussed prose writings in some detail. Confessing in one article to his fondness for the very name *essay* since he was a reader and writer of essays himself, he had "contracted a feeling of affectionate interest in and for the essayist and critic."[31]

In his best theoretical discussion, "Essay Writing.—The Champion" (the latter referring to Fielding's work by that name), Jones began by objecting to the argument of the reviewer in the London *Spectator* who maintained that the essay would gradually decline and disappear. He doubted that "the shortest, the most direct, the most personal, the most natural, form of prose-writing could ever become extinct, any more than letters, or songs, or oratory"—with all of which it "has much in common, and especially in its personal character, implying a familiarity, a mutual confidence and explicit directness, not to be attained in a higher and more ambitious form of composition." Like songs, essays contain "a certain lyrical spirit ... however homely and anti-poetical the essays may be," as Franklin's or "the second-rate papers of Hazlitt (who is hardly a fair instance, for he was a poet as much as Burke or Jeremy Taylor)." After citing the "poetic feeling" of Lamb and Emerson and the "fancy" of Hunt in their essays, he concluded that the essayist is "a humbler sort of bard, a prose lyrist, a writer of the walk of poetry, which Horace includes under the designation of *'musa pedestris.'* "

"Essays, too," Jones continued, "are very similar to letters, in their variety of topics; in their familiarity of address, and in the 'handling' or style." The writers of each are allowed "equal vanity, or egotism, or wise self-consideration, as you will"; there is room for sketches of character or manners, for satire or compliment, for philosophical discussion, "aesthetical analysis, or historical retrospect." The essay offers the writer the "widest allowable limits" of that freedom to say what one could not in the "ordinary intercourse of society" which Zimmermann called the great virtue of all writing: it restricts "the writer less in the development of his humors, whims, and agreeable prejudices upon paper than any other species of composition. It is indeed a mixed kind of writing, personal authorship, as free as possible from mere scholasticism or pedantry." And it is no nearer extinction now than in the days of Montaigne, though it may now treat different subjects, and be found in different places—in newspaper leaders, review articles, lectures, and passages of orations.

Advising essayists to stand up for their rights, he said that they have been "too long bullied by the long-winded historical novelists and reviewers, who think the essay contemptible from its brevity, certainly not from its subjects, nor yet from its execution." Americans who speak in this tone would do well to remember that our literature is "pre-eminently a periodical one thus far." Continuing Young America's interest in the newer shorter forms of literature, he defended all short forms. Writers of short pieces have often flown higher, though they do not stay so long on the wing as have the authors of long pieces: "A falcon is a nobler bird than the buzzard, who may be hovering over carrion all day..."[32]

Jones elaborated his definition of the essay by characterizing more fully certain subtypes. As might be expected from a Young American, he is most acute and thorough on the political pamphlet and political essay. Defending first the importance of political writings, he said that politics "is a theme of some dignity, perhaps of the greatest." And occasionally writers on political topics, who are also poets and philosophers, produce great and durable works. There are three classes of political writers:

   I. Those who write to and for statesmen and philosophers;
  II. They who write for those of the educated classes who are neither; and
 III. Those who write for that "many-headed monster," the people.

Certain qualities appropriate to each class are indicated by the qualities of the best English writers of each type: for the first, Burke's brilliance, profundity, and imaginative power; for the second, Junius's sarcasm and keen and pointed style; and the third, Paine's shrewd, clear, pithy, and caustic style.

In praising Paine, Jones discussed certain traits that all political writing should have: "always full of sense," he is "perfectly clear, and admirably concise"; but when he attempts it he is "as brilliant a declaimer as Burke, with almost equal fancy, and without any of his verbosity." Furthermore:

He has none of the common faults of political writers: he is never wordy—never clumsy and round-about in his expressions—never dull and tedious in his arguments. He has no pointless anecdotes—no heavy familiarity—no puerile rhetoric—no labored bombast. His sentences are clear and shapely—he is closely logical, and his arguments are connected as by a fine net-work. Whatever style he undertook, whether of expostulation or defence, narrative or logical, declamatory or moral, ironical or earnest, it always was perfectly perspicuous and admirably appropriate.[33]

Two other qualities of good political writing close Jones's description of the form. First, *"Personality* we affirm to be the most striking trait of the most brilliant political writing." The great political writer must be a violent partisan. Second, "in politics, as in most things, the most striking arguments are those *ad hominem* and *ad absurdum."* Of the latter we may observe that in a great many political arguments "a laugh is the best logic." Of the former: "The argument *ad hominem* affects a man's interest, and appeals to his pride or excites his indignation, and moves his feelings. It is the most effective argument to be used with the majority of men, and when enlivened by comic ridicule, or exaggerated into something like vituperative eloquence by the presence of a Juvenal tone of sarcastic rebuke, it displays the perfection of political satire ..." The wit of political writing must be based upon genuine knowledge and understanding: political wit, admitting of "little play of fancy, and few or no imaginative excursions," is only a livelier way of putting an argument. Reasoning by analogies, illustrations, "epigrammatic logic," Junius, Horn Tooke, Tom Paine, William

Hazlitt "sought to reach the *reductio ad absurdum* by the argument *ad hominem*. The accumulation of ridiculous traits of
character made up a comic picture, and demonstrated practical
absurdities in conduct at the same time. On the other hand, by
a process of exhaustive analysis, they *precipitated* (as a chemist
would say) the ludicrous points of a subject."[34] Such are the
general qualities of the political pamphlet and political writing
that Jones illustrated by detailed analyses of many writers.

A second subtype of the essay to which Jones gave attention
was the review article. "Review writing has now become an
art . . ." It has been "methodized into a system," with "its rules
and canons and peculiar style." Its analysis must be exhaustive
and thorough; its wit bright and " 'palpable' "; its logic close and
ingenious; and its rhetoric elaborate and dazzling. "The style
must never lag behind the story. There must be animation, at
all events . . . A flat reviewer, however accurate and true, must
fail; a true story does not answer the purpose . . . while a clever
conjecture passes for more than an acknowledged truth, which
wants the stimulus of novelty." Though this latter is not as it
should be, one need only read Macaulay, whose reviews are the
"very Iliad and Odyssey" of review writing, to be convinced of
the justice of the remark. More capable men have written review
articles but without his mastery of the art; Macaulay is "that
rare union of critic and miscellaneous writer—a critical essayist."[35]

While describing the characteristics of Edward Everett as a
writer and orator, Jones distinguished another form of the essay,
the literary address. Like the review, it "has become a classic
form of writing: a species of oratory the growth of the present
century." Less didactic than the lecture, "it is the elaborate eloquence of the fine scholar." A literary festival, an event in political history, or a eulogistic ceremony brings it forth.[36]

"Next to the essay," Jones wrote, "the letter is the most agreeable form of the minor literature." It is familiar and approaches

the closest to conversation. Authors of high pretension have often failed in this type of writing, which is built on the "plain ground of common-place reality." "Raillery" and "refined sentiment" are the most pleasing talents exhibited in letters. For his classification of kinds of letters, Jones drew upon James Howell: letters may be on any subject, "yet commonly they are either narratory, objurgatory, consolatory, monitory, or congratulatory." Howell, he added, dces not mention certain other types such as "ardent love letters," "purely literary letters," and "lively, gay epistles, that turn upon nothing."[37]

Jones began his discussion of the sermon and preaching in a harsh enough manner: "When we consider the frequency of the occasion, the nobleness of the topics, their supreme importance, the efficacy of the act well performed, the genius requisite, the variety of congregations, the number of preachers, we are at a complete stand to account for the deplorably low state of preaching." This low state can be traced to "a defect of literary accomplishment" among the clergy: "style and manner are not sufficiently attended to." Modern preachers, who do not realize that the sermon is a form of art, should turn to the old English Divines for their training. They should also attend to what Emerson says in his "Divinity School Address," in which occurs "the best definition of preaching we can recollect": " 'Preaching is the expression of the moral sentiment in application to the duties of life.' " What are the characteristics of a good sermon?

The style of sermons cannot be too plain and simple, in general. The text is perfectly clear and earnest. Strength and seriousness are the chief qualities. Let it be rather a labored plainness than a labored elegance. The greatest truths, like the richest gems, show best plain set. The best character, for a writer of sermons, is Ben Jonson's character of Cartwright, the Dramatist, who was also a Preacher. "He, my son Cartwright, writes all like a man." Joined to this manly sense let there be a liberal spirit of humanity, a sympathy with men as men; compassion and fellow-feeling.

To the youthful student of divinity Jones would say: "of the old Divines drink your fill—of wisdom, and fancy, and piety, and acute knowledge, and ability of every kind. What pictures, and fair conceits, and rich harmonies, in Taylor! what ingenious thoughts, so fine, so delicate, in Donne! what massy arguments in Barrow and Sherlock: and he that reads the contemporaries of these old masters, will confess them to have written as with a crisped pen."[38]

V

Of the topics and themes to which critics in the American reviews often turned, one of the most pervasive was the plea for a distinctive national literature in America. Most critics of the time wanted, in one sense, an American literature, that is, literature written by Americans. But not all were asking for a *distinctively American* literature, and the division of sentiment followed more or less political lines. The conservative Whig journals cared little about developing a "truly" national literature; liberal Democratic journals called again and again for a new and different American literature. And among the liberal magazines the *Democratic Review,* in articles written by Young Americans, was especially persistent. The dividing line between the two points of view followed, we may observe also, the course of the line between the conservative "Romantics" and the progressive "Romantics." Young America tended simply to extend the Utilitarian view, cited earlier, that there must be "a New Literature to fit the New Man in the New Age"—in a New Country.

We may see the contrasting attitudes in brief form in the reviews of Catherine Maria Sedgwick's books in the conservative *New York Review* and in the *Democratic Review.* The *New York Review* found Miss Sedgwick's *Means and Ends* a pleasing book in some ways, but, as in all her recent books, "a tinge of *Radicalism* runs through the book; or rather, and which we dislike still more, an appearance of quiet taking-for-granted that ultra-democratic sentiments are the only philanthropic ones." Its review of *Live and Let Live* objected also to the *"ultra-democratic* sentiments": the people should be instructed in the duties of liberty, not the rights; too easily the people develop "the licentious spirit of *Liberty above Law,* begetting discontent with established and necessary distinctions and subordinations, and hatred towards the richer classes." It felt that the "democratic element" should be restrained, purified, and guided into "safe and rational channels." And in her advice to servants, Miss Sedgwick forgets where the blame lies in employer-employee troubles today: "We do not believe the fault is wholly or chiefly on the side of the employers."[39]

The *Democratic*'s review is in decidedly different terms. *Means and Ends,* though it is an unpretentious little book, is a "contribution to our American literature." As the reviewer defends his statement, we see what "American literature" meant to the Young Americans and the *Democratic*. The critic took his greatest pleasure in looking at the qualities which the *New York Review* scorned: the "ultra-democratic" tone and sentiment. He liked the book's "thoroughly *American* and Democratic—words that we regard as altogether synonymous—character."[40] Thus we see that for Young America, in simple terms, "American literature" meant "Democratic literature." And one gathers that the reiteration of a call for an American literature of this sort by the political radicals and liberals, if for no other reason, led to the opposition to the plea from those on the conservative Whig side of the fence. The Democrats had preëmpted the theme: the *Whig Review*'s comment on Whipple's praise of American authors is typical. Whipple was said to prefer, other things being equal, an American book to a foreign one: "We are almost afraid to say this, lest we should be thought to disparage him ..." But Whipple's subjects of eulogy are safe

Whigs—"Daniel Webster and Rufus Choate; noble themes!"[41]

Young America and the *Democratic Review* became, then, probably the most strenuous advocates in America of this sort of new and distinctive American literature. Almost every aspect of the things which characterized them led to their emphasis upon American literature. Their belief in the "Manifest Destiny" of America, their interest in finding the spirit of Democracy in literature and in developing a literature for the people, and their consciousness of the writing talent enrolled in the Democratic Party were particularly important in influencing their point of view. But since they usually equated an American and a democratic literature and we have already seen their call for a democratic literature, we need illustrate only briefly their activities as literary nationalists.[42]

It must not be forgotten that Young America did not publish all its literary criticism in the *Democratic,* though this was its most important organ. *Arcturus,* the *Boston Miscellany* after *Arcturus* merged with it, the *Literary World* when it was edited by the Duyckincks, the various South Carolina magazines with which Simms was connected, and other magazines, contain their "Very-Americanism." E. A. Duyckinck was even able to insert Young American sentiments into one review of Cornelius Mathews in the Whig *New York Review:* he called for a great American poet and a great American humorous writer, asserting that "no nation can ever be truly respected by others, or know rightly how to respect itself, without a national literature." Maintaining that it was "in vain that a nation is said to live epic poems, if they do not write them," he wished the new national literature to express the "spirit of the age."[43] But this is an anomaly in the *New York Review,* as it would have been also in the later *Whig Review,* which campaigned vigorously against the idea of a national literature. To the *Democratic* we may turn again for Young America's most characteristic views.

Young America in the *Democratic* was not sure whether there was or was not an American literature already in existence. When pleading in the abstract for a more thoroughly democratic and American literature, it was inclined to say that America had no national literature. But in other places, when specific writers were being reviewed, it tended to assume that there was already a distinctive national literature: it should merely be more so. In the "Introduction" to the first number, the flat statement was: "we have no national literature." We have, it explained, only pale imitations embodying the aristocratic spirit of English literature; we must create a new literature filled with the "animating spirit" of our democracy. The antidemocratic spirit of our literature must be changed, for it is "poisoning at the spring the young mind of our people." "Our 'better educated classes' drink in an anti-democratic habit of feeling and thinking from the copious, and it must be confessed delicious, fountain of the literature of England; they give the same spirit to our own, in which we have little or nothing that is truly democratic and American." The "Introduction" closed with the declaration that one purpose of the *Democratic Review* would be to vindicate "the true glory and greatness of the democratic principle, by infusing it into our literature."[4]

In a similar vein, but more rhetorical, was the plea in "The Great Nation of Futurity," probably written by O'Sullivan. "And our literature!—Oh, when will it breathe the spirit of our republican institutions? When will it be imbued with the God-like aspiration of intellectual freedom—the elevating principle of equality? When will it assert *its* national independence, and speak the soul—the heart of the American people? Why cannot our literati comprehend the matchless sublimity of our position amongst the nations of the world—our high destiny..." Our scenery, our private life, our public life are fit subjects for literature. "Why, then, do our authors aim at no higher degree of merit, than a successful imitation of English writers of celebrity?"[45]

Other articles with a less demanding tone may be represented by the review of two collections of American poetry. The reviewer was pleased "with the signs of literary progress." But "we have formed so exalted an idea of what the literature of this nation should be, that we are not easily satisfied." We must "go ahead" to further achievements before we may lay claim to "having a distinct national literature" which expresses fully the genius of our people.[46]

But the best, the most ably reasoned and learned, of the more temperate pleas for nationality in literature came in 1847 in a series of three articles (which picked up one of Griswold's anthologies in mid-course to treat it to a slashing). The articles are partly answers to the two leading conservative reviews, the *Whig Review* and the *North American,* which had been alleging that the literary nationalists had no real conception of what a national literature should be.

E. W. Johnson and C. W. Webber in the *Whig* had been particularly violent in their objections. Johnson confessed that "we never were able to conceive" what they who talk of an American literature mean. There is nothing new in American thought to be expressed. And the only new literary vehicles into which the old ideas may be put are those used by authors "who degrade and vulgarize the tongue and taste of the country ... by their adoption of a particular local slang" (such as Major Jack Downing and Sam Slick): these are not models for "a new and noble literature" in the future. "When these things shall found for us a learning, the Ethiopian Minstrels will create for us a Music, and the disciples of Jim Crow a Theatre of our own." (Said the *Alleghanian:* "Are they [Jack Downing and Sam Slick] models? No, but they are grit rock out of which models will be hewn. Shall they 'found for us a learning'? A Learning! No, they will not found for us a learning; but the time will come, when we will have to found a learning for them.") All our "ancestral memories," Johnson went on, are still English; "our laws, too, and our very politics breathe scarcely less than our historic recollections and all our literary associations of the mother-country." We must conclude that there is nothing from within literature itself or from society without that can or should give us a new literature. The puffers of American literature have "by no means given themselves the trouble to inquire" what they mean by American literature.[47]

C. W. Webber treated the subject with the wild abandon of the very "Young Giant," the Yankee Jonathan, the "Democratic scion of the Titans," that he condemned. He listed the "assailable points in our Native literary character," among which exaggeration bulked large. But, with broad irony, he says that "Finnicking Conservatism" should not protest "when the Sovereigns choose to amuse themselves with boxing thunder-snags, swallowing greased lightning, or drinking the beds of rivers dry." Conservatives are foolish to be incredulous about "those eminently classic contests between that modern Centaur, 'the Half-Horse and Half-Alligator' and some Feline Lapithae—known in the vulgate as Wild-cat or Panther! Pshaw! the 'unterrified Democracy!'—what can it not do?" American authors are "Native" in only one thing: nothing could be more truly cool and Yankee than the marvelous skill at stealing of a few native authors who work "for the benefit of the literature of 'the Model Republic.' "[48]

It was to such attacks as these that the Young American reviewer in the *Democratic* (almost certainly E. A. Duyckinck, in the first two articles) addressed himself. He began by tracing the historical reasons for the retarded and colonial status of our literature: the subjection to England, the necessity to tame the country, and the like. Building upon the principles of Madame de Staël, Jeffrey, and others, he then explained "the idea and the necessity of nationality": "First and foremost, nationality involves the idea of home writers. Secondly, the choice of a due proportion of home themes, affording opportunity for descriptions of our scenery, for the illustration of passing events, and the preservation of what tradition has rescued from the past, and for the exhibition of the manners of the people, and the circumstances which give form and pressure to the time and the spirit of the country; and all these penetrated and vivified by an intense and enlightened patriotism." A review of authorities—among others Madame de Staël, Bacon, Montesquieu, Schlegel—makes clear the worth of the idea. It should be obvious, the reviewer continued, that "our view of nationality is conceived in no narrow spirit. Illiberality and exclusiveness have no part in our creed. We would burn no books, banish no authors, shut our hearts against no appeal which speaks to them in the voice of nature. We would not narrow, but enlarge, the horizon of letters; we would not restrict the empire of thought, but annex our noble domain to it." And we would certainly disagree with the learned *North American Review* in its objection to literary nationalism. Contrary to the belief of the *North American,* a national self-consciousness does not hinder the development of genius in literature. "We would ask ... under what reigns was the national spirit of England ... raised to a loftier tone, than during the reign of Elizabeth, and the period of the Commonwealth, under Cromwell ... ?" And did not Bacon, Shakespeare, and Milton live at that time? At any rate: "It poorly comports with our lofty assertion of national superiority, or with even an ordinary and just sense of self-respect, to be dependent for the intellectual aliment of the people ... upon foreign writers ... who often, in obedience to the influences which surround them, write in a spirit not only alien, but positively hostile to our people, our institutions and national character."[49]

The second and third parts of the discussion were somewhat

diverted from the main point of issue as the reviewer stopped to object to Griswold's *Prose Writers of America* (which contained the attack on Young America noted earlier), but the main purpose was achieved: to "point out the American writers and writings most deeply imbued with a national spirit." Bancroft, Irving (for what he had written of this country), Cooper, Miss Sedgwick, Simms, and Cornelius Mathews were instanced in the second part of the discussion (Mathews receiving a lion's share of the attention).[50] The third of the series, by a different hand, continued the slashing of Griswold and added to the list of truly American writers that Griswold might have included in his volume: for example, where, he asked, are Thomas Paine and William Leggett and Edward Livingston?[51]

The final comment of the *Democratic Review* that we may notice seems to show that it felt that some progress had been made by 1849. It rejoiced: "With so able and enterprising a publisher as Mr. Putnam, the vague idea, indistinctly entertained by a few individuals among us, that there is no American literature, is likely soon to be extinguished." It believed that the United States was growing out of its colonial status. The Revolution of seventy years ago brought political independence; the "Revolution of 1837" freed the country from "the bondage of paper credits." "The next step now apparently being taken is literary emancipation . . ."[52]

VI

Young America and the *Democratic Review,* along with nearly all the other critics and magazines of the day, insisted upon moral purity in literature; indeed, cognizant of the charges of moral delinquency often urged against liberal and radical Jeffersonians and Jacksonians, the more politically minded Young Americans, like O'Sullivan, seemed to go out of their way to do so. Their more or less Utilitarian emphasis upon the usefulness of literature and the necessity for truth in literature led also to their insistence. Nesbitt's statement about the *Westminster Review* may be applied to the *Democratic:* "Thus in the literary department as elsewhere the reviewers nourished Philistinism among undiscriminating middle-class readers." O'Sullivan and others were quite capable of echoing the sentiments of the anonymous reviewer of Gibbon: *"Genius,* mysterious and all-pervading as is its power, cannot change the unalterable distinctions of right and wrong, or annihilate the everlasting relations of man to his maker." We may be sure that "society has interests more vital, infinitely more important, than the gratification of *taste,* or the pleasures of the imagination." The reviewer quoted Schiller's lament: "Oh, that *greatness* always were *good,* that *goodness* always were great!"[53]

But the prevailing opinion of the Democratic Young Americans was on the side of liberality. John Bigelow's two articles of attack upon Charles Anthon's classical dictionary show its point of view. One of Bigelow's major objections to Anthon's dictionary was its narrow standard of morality and the approval of that standard in the journals and reviews (particularly the Whig *New York Review,* mentioned by name). Bigelow began:

We find our author repeatedly declaring, and his declarations echoed with accumulated emphasis through our journals and Reviews, that this Dictionary is to contain nothing in the slightest degree offensive to the youth of either sex—that no paragraph therein contained shall bring the blush to the chastest cheek, or violate the most fastidious delicacy. What amount of "grossness" is legitimate within the above limitation it is difficult to define; nor do we see what particular propriety there can be in selecting the extra class of a fashionable boarding-school, or the *précieuses ridicules* of a "reading society for mutual improvement," to define to us the jurisdiction which our memories shall retain over the moral conduct of our ancestors.

A history of mythology, said Bigelow, cannot be truthfully written on such a principle. "We protest against emasculating history for the purposes of favoring the prudery or tickling the moral

self-complacency of any class or sect. A fact, wherever and whenever and however begotten, should be inviolable. The interests
of the whole should never be sacrificed in protecting a few
morally deformed from temptation." Bigelow then instanced
falsifications for the sake of purity in Anthon's work.[54]

The New York *New World* in an editorial undoubtedly by
Anthon defended the dictionary from the attacks of the *Democratic:* "Gracious Heaven! Are we to be told ... by this advocate
of obscenity, that it is wrong to conceal from the view of the
young the horrid impurities of heathenism?" Of one example
of suppression cited by Bigelow, the *New World* exclaimed
further: "Good God! To talk thus of a woman who exhibited her
naked person on a public stage ..." And the *Democratic* has the
effrontery to quote "with an air of complacency the infamous
defence of obscenity by the sceptic Bayle."[55]

Bigelow returned to the attack with another article in a later
number of the *Democratic*. On morality he did little more than
reiterate his previous stand. He did add that "Dr. Anthon does
not appear to be aware of the difference between exposing the
immorality of the ancients and justifying it."[56]

The liberal attitude of Young America as seen in the *Democratic* may be further illustrated by the comments of W. A.
Jones upon morality in literature. He entered the subject from
a consideration of children's books. He stated flatly: "Most tale-
writers are altogether too didactic." With Poe (whom he does
not mention here), he felt that the effect of the work is lost when
it becomes a lecture or a sermon. "There are two ethical questions
to be considered in books of entertainment for children, and indeed for readers of all ages. Should the work be based, or com-
posed, on moral grounds, i.e., as directly teaching any peculiar
system of morality or religion? And should each work have a
palpable moral aim? We do not speak of the tendency of such
works: that, it is fairly implied, ought to be good invariably."

But the morality should not be "palpably stamped" on the work. The best people do not need or desire "to be continually dosed with panaceas of ethical disquisitions or tirades upon religion, in however small quantities." The proper place for such things is not in "an episode of a tale or the preface to a novel." Certainly a moral purpose, "explicitly set forth," is of "very doubtful utility."

Coleridge, that most spiritual of Poets and purest of men, thought a poem ought to be aimless, just in the same view and for the precise reason that the finest female character was characterless. It would require a distinct essay to follow out the ramifications of this principle, but the intelligent reader will appreciate its truth. Honest, liberal-minded Mrs. Barbauld taxed him for the want of a moral aim in his Ancient Mariner, which very deficiency he considered a merit. And in a liberal sense, it is such, though it is given to few to see why—a true moral it had, but not an avowed moral end. To delight was its original duty, but nothing delights the pure except purity itself: hence, it inculcated a valuable lesson without seeming to teach at all.

The popular feeling, the Young American had to admit, is with Mrs. Barbauld; and for the "common sense of mankind . . . we entertain a sincere respect." Yet here Coleridge was correct. Hazlitt advocated the same side of the question, and "where the finest poet and the acutest critic agree" we must yield. Today a "disagreeable moral pedantry spoils some delightful books"; the "whole herd of religious novelists and moral tale-writers" "ignorantly and repeatedly" err in this respect.[57]

Young America in the *Democratic* would generally have agreed with Jones: there should not be an obtrusive, simple moral in literature. They would have agreed with the anonymous writer of a notice of *Undine* who wanted a "moral" of a very comprehensive sort: "We were about to call this a moral tale, but a German scholar tells us that the original word which is translated moral, signifies literally 'life knowledge.' Now all this is conveyed to us in that rich, abundant word *moral,* but the reader may think of Aesop's Fables and the Rambler, an obtrusive common-place moral, which is a very different thing—so we use the German phrase as an illustration of our meaning. This book is full of the best 'life-knowledge.' "[58]

VII

In 1847, four years after the theoretical foundation for Young America's Locofoco politico-literary system had been well laid, a reviewer of Emerson in the *Democratic Review* wrote one sentence that summarized, in tone and substance, much that Young America had to say about literature: "We would that the poet stood very near to the throbbing heart of humanity, and were wholly inspired by the high hopes with which the race is stirred."[59] The Young American *critic*, too, we should remember, felt that he should address the "throbbing heart of humanity," the heart and intellect of the "reading democracy." It was this attitude that provoked the *Whig Review* to scornful remarks on "learned authors" who, "in deference to the spirit of the age," write "to instruct the multitude," or "that utilitarian school of critics, who ... would, without compunction, convert the Parthenon into a Fourierite quadrangle."[60]

To this democratic "spirit of the age," we may also turn as one explanation for Young America's neglect of certain literary questions that the conservatives tried to answer. Young America had little to say about the "art" of poetry on which Poe built his familiar definitions of poetry. And it seldom concerned itself with an attempt to define the process by which the poet symbolized the "hopes," the "ideas," the "spirit" that it asked the poet to express. The conservative reviewers in the *Whig Review*, less concerned about the "spirit of the age," dealt with this problem more often: they more often defined poetry as, in the words of Henry Norman Hudson, an "organic unity" of thought and image, created by the poet who sees "the facts and forms of nature" as symbolic and who "thus speaks in symbols, instead of propositions."[61] Young America would have agreed. Even while calling for the poet to concern himself with the spirit of the age in the review cited above, it chided Emerson for neglecting the "art" of composition in his desire to present "undisciplined, untrimmed nature"; it added that when the poet who does not have the genius of Emerson lays aside "all thought of means" and tries to "make every verse a surprise," he "can make every verse a very disagreeable surprise indeed."[62] But it felt that the American critic had more pressing obligations to society than to explain to it the "symbolic process" or the art of "the rhythmical creation of beauty."

We may notice finally that Young America's emphasis upon the social obligation of the poet and the critic, whatever the peculiar national variations in the common beliefs about literature, is strikingly similar to that found in a typical middle-class English periodical of the same period. Leslie A. Marchand might be describing the criticism of the New York periodicals instead of that in the *Athenaeum* of the early Victorian age in the following words:

Perhaps the sharpest line of demarcation between the earlier Romantic movement (during the first three decades of the nineteenth century) and Victorian Romanticism is to be found in the active desire and attempt of the latter to apply its intuitional knowledge to social rather than individual uses. The poet, the seer, then becomes the prophet of "progress," on every plane, because his mind has contact with eternal truth. This was the highest function of all literature, to find in the deep well of creative imagination, which was fed from the purest sources of nature, the water of life for a spiritual-social regeneration, the belief in which was a common denominator of the Victorian mind.[63]

Obviously, conservative Whigs preferred that the regeneration brought by literature should be spiritual, Young America that it be social.

CHAPTER V

YOUNG AMERICA'S CRITICAL JUDGMENTS

I

YOUNG AMERICAN literary critics were all practical and practicing critics who concerned themselves not only with theoretical critical systems, but also with applying their critical assumptions and principles to specific authors and their works. Though a knowledge of their basic premises may lead one to predict with some degree of accuracy what they are likely to say about any author, one cannot understand their criticism without some information about their specific critical judgments. The account which follows attempts to suggest—not detail—what Young Americans said about specific authors and to show to what writers their "tastes" and principles drew them.

As their most representative periodical, the *Democratic Review* will again provide us the basic pattern of their critical judgments. In *Arcturus*, the *Broadway Journal*, the *Boston Miscellany*, the *Union Magazine*, the *Pathfinder*, the *Church Record*, the *Churchman*, the *New Yorker*, the *Literary World*, *Holden's Dollar Magazine*, *Yankee Doodle*, the *Elephant*, even in the *New York Review*, and the *Whig Review*, as well as others, may be found Young American critical judgments to which we may occasionally turn to complete the pattern; but we need do so only occasionally, because the volume of their work for the *Democratic* makes it representative—more than merely representative at times, since W. A. Jones, in particular, often pieced together earlier articles from *Arcturus* and elsewhere to sell again to the *Democratic*.

II

Probably because they could find few democratically inclined non-English poets, Young America and the *Democratic Review* seldom turned to poets of continental Europe or the classical past. Most of the reviews of such poets in the *Democratic* whose authors can be identified are not by critics closely related to Young America. The young T. W. Higginson reviewed Sappho; L. F. Tasistro wrote long articles on Goethe and Schiller; an unidentified reviewer discussed modern Spanish poetry.[1] The reviews of Petrarch, Alfieri, and Béranger are more Young American in tone and show to what use Young America wished to put poetry.

The *Democratic* was in one of its more Utilitarian or "Victorian" or Philistine moods when it discussed Petrarch. What is Petrarch to those who seek a progressive, new poetry for the new American age? He was a "false priest, a negligent father," a friend who always had some personal end in view; he might have raised a family which would have leavened the depravity of the times, but "he ran after laurel crowns, and danced attendance on emperors and nobles, dawdling on in endless verse about Laura, and pedantic epistles to Virgil and Quintilian, and others equally effective to contemporary princes, popes and tribunes." With hardly any encouragement he nourished a love for fifty years, certainly wholly contrary to sense, reason, and propriety. Poetry on such a subject can never be truly popular in America. This may be contrasted with the *Whig Review*'s approving sentimental sketch on the romantic life of Petrarch by H. T. Tuckerman, whose tone may be assumed from the interesting but rather baffling statement that "Petrarch was true to Love, and developed its elements more richly through solitude."[2]

J. T. Headley, a member of Young America's mutual admi-

---

[1] For notes to chapter v see pages 139–140.

ration society, commended Alfieri for his interest in fighting tyranny. But Alfieri should have been more direct in his efforts: instead of writing drama, "he should have been the *nation's bard,* and spoken to the heart of the people in plain earnest language." Béranger had obvious qualities that would appeal to the *Democratic Review,* and it discovered them. It pointed out that Béranger had said, " 'My muse is the *peuple,'* " and that he had converted the song into a composition able to carry more than wine and love as subjects: "Song . . . is the organ of the masses." His poetry is written in a style which clothes "with admirable expression, the hopes, the wishes, and the mournful regrets of a whole nation."[3]

No critical essays on the earlier English poets appeared in the *Democratic Review* until toward the end of the fifth volume. And then a critic, probably E. A. Duyckinck, found a suitable topic. His title was "America and the Early English Poets," an unimportant article which quoted the poetical comments of Spenser, Drayton, Daniel, Herbert, Marvell, and Berkeley on America.[4] It is cited here because it represents an interest of the more literary of the Young Americans which is not adequately represented in the *Democratic Review.* Young America, like the New England transcendentalists, found much to its liking in the seventeenth-century English religious poets.

In the *New York Review, Arcturus,* the *Church Record,* the *Churchman,* the *Whig Review,* and elsewhere, Duyckinck and Jones reviewed such poets as Herbert, the Fletchers, Donne, Vaughan, Quarles, and Crashaw. Duyckinck's article on Herbert is typical of his essays. The religious strain in Herbert endeared him to Episcopalian Duyckinck and the Episcopalian *New York Review.* Herbert, he wrote, "cast his glance not towards Parnassus, but Zion." His literary merit "lies in sentiment always ardent and sincere, uttered in bold language, and unfrequently adorned by a vigorous fancy." Though many of his conceits seemed "low" to Duyckinck, many could be justified: in "A True Hymn" we may see "the mode in which a mere conceit can come to the aid of a serious thought." Even the unusual imagery and the rugged lines serve a purpose in Herbert's poetry: "Perhaps the frequent ruggedness of the line or remoteness of the conceit and imagery aids this devotional feeling: the sense is not rounded in a couplet, to be passed over by the mind in the cadence of a period; but we pause and think while the moral finds its way to the soul."[5]

Referring to this essay of Duyckinck's and others in *Arcturus,* Jones wrote an article about Quarles and Crashaw for the *Whig Review,* which may represent his critical judgments on the writers of this period. Quarles, he believed, does not deserve to be forgotten: much of his poetry is "sententious and dogmatical, full of thought and serious feeling. The style is as hard as enamel and as polished, pointed to conciseness, and weighty with the dignity of religious truth." The neglect of Crashaw, said Jones, is even more remarkable. The religious verse of Montgomery is known to everyone, while Crashaw, "infinitely the superior of Montgomery," is scarcely familiar even by name. ("Montgomery bears to Crashaw about the relation that Pollok may be said to sustain to Milton.") The conceits and oddities of style of Crashaw, Donne, Herbert, Quarles, the Fletchers, and Cowley should not frighten the reader from their great poetry. In Crashaw, as a matter of fact, there is more "really admirable poetry" "than can be furnished out of any popular poet in England of the present day, except Wordsworth." In his great admiration for Crashaw, Jones even disagreed with his critical mentor Hazlitt, but he was able to excuse Hazlitt: "Hazlitt has spoken ignorantly of the 'hectic manner' of Crashaw. We suspect he knew him only by report."[6]

If seventeenth-century religious poets were not found suitable for the *Democratic Review,* Restoration and eighteenth-century poets were—and the amount of attention devoted to these writers is, so far as I know, unique in the periodicals of the time. W. A. Jones, in the course of his series on political writers, looked at the satire of Dryden, Swift, and Churchill, later discussed Blackmore and Akenside as literary physicians, and Dryden and Pope as writers of poetical epistles. Satire, Jones said, is essentially "unpoetical": it "tends to diminish and degrade, whereas true poetry aims to exalt and refine"; yet its practical value is great and next to that of religion. Calling Dryden the head of satirists in time and excellence, he said that Dryden had created in the characters of Absalom, Achitophel, and Zimri of his masterpiece "classic portraits" that surpass those of Pope. Swift of course is of little significance as a writer of poetry; Churchill, with much of Dryden's talent for portraits and passionate declamation, was more dashing, careless, and hasty than Dryden. Blackmore had some talent for the "piebald species of didactic writing, half prose, half rhyme," called philosophical poetry in his time, "but for higher philosophical poetry, he was about as fit as the coachman that drove his lumbering old chariot." Jones professed never to have heard of or met "a hearty lover of Akenside's poetry," which has "power and philosophical precision" but is lacking in "nature, freshness, unconscious grace." Finally, of Dryden and Pope as letter writers: "The finest writers of poetical epistles in the English language, are those two fine poets, to whom continual reference is made of necessity whenever we wish to find the most graceful specimens of elegant compliment, or classic enthusiasm of eulogy, or to read the neatest or the most forcible satirical touches; whom we turn to for the finest judgment or the most ardent sentiment; whose works are models of rhetoric and versification; and who, if not great poets, were admirable writers of verse—Pope and Dryden."[7]

But it is not to these writers of the more distant past that the *Democratic* and Young America gave most attention: they looked to poets of the immediate past, the present, and the future (the coming Homer of the mass). While the Whigs in the *New York* and *Whig* reviews dignified Wordsworth and Coleridge with full reviews, Young Americans, without denying the greatness of these poets, found it more politic to concentrate upon Shelley. They discussed all the important English poets of the Romantic period, as in the two articles summarizing Margaret Fuller's criticism of the "Sacred Nine"; they even picked up such unfamiliar poets as the Scotch Motherwell (a poet of the people partly spoiled by that "night-mare idea," his "High-Toryism"); but their criticism of Wordsworth and Shelley is most typical.⁸

Wordsworth, and the admission was hard to make, would not do. Jones called Wordsworth a great poet in his own province of "profoundly meditative and philosophical poetry," but as a popular poet for the people he lacked enthusiasm, "the storm and tempest of passion," which Byron, for example, possessed (though Jones recorded his personal preference for Wordsworth). Furthermore, "full of human sympathy as is the poetry of this great master, it is the felling [*sic*] and compassion of a superior, not of an equal." He found "no democracy in his verse." Another critic, probably O'Sullivan, objected strenuously to Wordsworth's sonnets in defense of capital punishment; he could not deny the great genius of Wordsworth, *but* "we regret profoundly that Wordsworth should have lent the aid of his genius and his moral influence to promote this unholy purpose." The "strongly conservative cast of his mind and political opinions" has misled him.⁹

On the basis of Parke Godwin's essay on Shelley in the *Democratic Review,* Miss Julia Power, in her history of Shelley's reputation in America, regards Godwin as the "best Shelley critic" of the years from 1830 to 1850 and "one of the best of the century." However that may be, his essay is a striking example of the Young American politico-literary system at work. It is a thorough treatment of Shelley more in the mode of the quarterly review article than was common in the *Democratic Review*. His point of view was, of course, that of a reforming, democratic "Romanticist," a fact which goes far to explain his approval of Shelley. He began in traditional review manner with a survey of Shelley's life, turned next to the poetry, finally to "the man." Godwin listed quite systematically the faults and virtues of Shelley as a poet. Certain defects in "the structure of his mind" led to his use of a peculiar and vague diction, which was often a sign of vagueness in his thought. His descriptions lack "actuality," are too often enveloped in a hazy atmosphere, and, at other times, "possess too much of dazzling glare and splendor." Another fault, his obscurity, arose from "the exceeding subjectivity of his mind, and the exquisite delicacy of his imagination." He transferred the operations of his mind to those of nature, as when he compared the avalanche to the thought, not the thought to the avalanche. His virtue consisted, first, in his high conception of the "true function and destiny of a Poet." The preëminent characteristics of his poetry are its "imaginative power" and its "glowing spirit of freedom and love." In the last part of his essay Godwin is particularly concerned to establish Shelley's gentle, essentially religious nature.

Thus did Godwin attempt to accomplish the good Young American aim with which he prefaced his essay. It is the "destiny" of America to "teach the world what men have been among its brightest ornaments and worthiest benefactors." "It is reserved for America to rescue . . . Shelley's fame from the cold neglect which it is the interest of older nations to gather round it, and to show mankind, by her warm appreciation of his genius and character, how much virtue and excellence were lost when he perished."[10]

When they turned to contemporary English poets, Young America and the *Democratic Review* disagreed over ranking them by merit. To Tennyson, Elizabeth Barrett, and P. J. Bailey they gave the honor of long critical reviews, but Duyckinck, reviewing Barrett in the *Whig,* reported that the Horatian standard which excluded mediocrity would permit only Tennyson and Barrett to be called poets—and she is a better representative of the feminine character than he of the masculine. In the *Democratic,* however, Jones, judging by the "Miltonic standard," found that the only living poet was Wordsworth of the older generation: "a lower standard would admit Hunt, Proctor, Tennyson, Elizabeth Barrett; a lower deep (still far from low) would include Elliott, Milnes, Mrs. Norton. In a small class of poetic wits, may be placed Hood, Praed, and a few others. As classical copyists, Talfourd, Knowles, and Nelson Coleridge, deserve a respectable place: while Sir Edward Bulwer Lytton and Satan Montgomery would lead off a file of poetasters, writers of philosophic verse, and mystical transcendentalists, to the lowest pit of the critical Tartarus, there to endure the pangs and agony of damned authors and hopeless projectors."[11]

Wherever in the scale they might be put, Young America did agree that Tennyson and Barrett were of considerable merit; and their judgment was shared by the Whig reviews also. Duyckinck reviewed Cornelius Mathews's edition of Barrett in glowing terms for the *Whig;* Mathews did the honors for his own edition in the *Democratic.* Fanny Kemble Butler praised Tennyson in the *Democratic,* and C. A. Bristed and E. P. Whipple puffed him for the *Whig.*

But when Young America turned to P. J. Bailey and certain poets for the people like Ebenezer Elliott, the conservatives preferred not to follow. Henry Norman Hudson thoroughly dissected P. J. Bailey's *Festus* for the *Whig Review,* objecting to its liberal and transcendental philosophy, its liberal and democratic politics. The *Democratic* conceded that as a work of art *Festus* was wanting in a unified plan of development. "On the other hand, there are passages ... alive with the very soul of poetry, instinct with celestial fire, strong, deep, intense—worthy of the masters of song ..." And the "intended moral" of the work— "the ultimate triumph of good through evil"—is a sound one. W. A. Jones called Elliott, Miller, and Clare the most distinguished of the living poets of the people in England. Elliott is the "Poet for the People, *par excellence*": "He is one of the very foremost men of England, at this present writing, and a bard of nature's own making. A manly writer, full of true feeling; a poet of vast pathetic power in the drama of daily life, simple and sincere—an English Burns, without his lighter and gayer gifts; more domestic and religious, yet scornful and satirical in the right place, though affectionate and merciful to the erring." Quoting from J. B. Auld in *Arcturus,* Jones justified Elliott's themes as of as much heroic, tragic, and dramatic stature as those of the older poets: "this national starvation is no unheroic matter."[12]

The *Whig* and the *Democratic* were in sharp disagreement on American poets also. The prevailing opinion on American poets, particularly the younger American poets, in the *Whig* is well summed up in two short notices of volumes of poetry. Viewing the whole field of modern poetry with a skeptical eye, it could go no further than to say: "In these days of false poetry, transcendental and other, we are glad to praise what is attempted to be done in a right way, and is rather negatively deficient than positively vicious." It combined with this attitude another which grew out of its conservative political outlook. The reason it gave for commending the poetry of W. T. Bacon summarizes this attitude: "One feature, we may be permitted ... to commend in his poetical works, and that is that they express a purely poetical phase of imagination, and do not convert the winged genius of verse from its aerial functions to be the trumpeter of vain philosophy and false pathos. When Mr. B. writes a poem he writes it as a poet, and not as a humanitarian preacher, or a socialist lecturer. There is not a single poem on Labor in the whole book, which seems to be a very sure indication that the poet is himself a laborer in his vocation."[13] This point of view was hardly in harmony with the "spirit of the age."

The Young Americans writing for the *Democratic Review* felt that spirit of the age, and no doubt the flattering attention that the *Democratic* paid to American poets had something to do with the jaundiced eye with which the *Whig* regarded them. The *Democratic* followed quite well the typically Young American advice of Melville in Duyckinck's *Literary World:* "let America first praise mediocrity even, in her own children, before she praises . . . the best excellence in the children of any other land"; let America praise "those writers who breathe that unshackled democratic spirit of Christianity in all things." "And if any of our authors fail, or seem to fail, then, in the words of my Carolina cousin . . . , let us clap him on the shoulder, and back him against all Europe for his second round."[14]

The *Democratic Review* strained manfully from the beginning to praise even mediocre American poetry. And, surely, it had to search rather widely to find a suitable American poem to praise in its first number: it fastened upon *Miriam, a Dramatic Poem,* the "chief charm" of which was "the gentle tone of moral and religious beauty" which pervaded it. Its opinion of the work was recorded in definite terms: "We look upon 'Miriam' as an important accession to the poetic literature, not alone of our country, but of our language,—as a jewel of great price." And through the whole course of the magazine there were similar jewels backed against Europe. John Howard Payne puffed William Martin Johnson as one of "Our Neglected Poets" and projected a series of articles under the same title (but got no farther than the first one). Park Benjamin surveyed "Recent American Poetry," placing Bryant at the head of American poets, Halleck

and Sprague next, with Prentice, Willis, Sargent, and Dawes
following and G. Hill bringing up the rear ("Mr. Hill has cour-
age enough, but lacks strength"). Parke Godwin and H. T.
Tuckerman wrote separate review articles on Democratic Bryant
as the greatest American poet (the *Whig* had no article on
Bryant), but Godwin put Bryant not with the great giants
Spenser, Shakespeare, and Milton, but with Thomson, Cowper,
and Wordsworth. Another critic of "American Poetry" called
the "effusions" of early Colonial poets interesting as exhibitions
of the spirit of the times rather than as poems; more recent
American poets start off with Bryant at the top, Dana next, and
others beneath them in no particular order, Halleck, Sprague,
Willis, Sands, Pierpont, Wilcox, and Very. In "Poetry of the
West" the *Democratic* said the appropriate things about the
rising literature of the West which was destined to be more
truly American and democratic than that of any other section of
the country ("Verily, indeed, the star of empire seems determined
never to stop on its westward way") and praised especially a
labor poem by W. D. Gallagher. S. D. Langtree discovered that
Longfellow had been given a portion of the sacred fire, but he
is imitative and has the "unfortunate peculiarity" of putting
"but *one* idea" in each poem. The critic of Lucy Hooper could
not go through with the harsh critical plucking of her delicate
flowers, saying, "we abandon the design with which we began,"
and gave selections for the reader to judge for himself. Alexander
H. Everett, the Democratic Everett, looked upon Mrs. Sigourney
as "the first of the lady-poets of our country": and made the
cautious observation: "If her powers of expression were equal
to the purity and elevation of her habits of thought and feeling,
she would be a female Milton, or a Christian Pindar."[15]

The review of a Young American's book by two of the most
important Young Americans, Mathews by O'Sullivan and Duyckinck, is an example of the *Review* at its most Democratic and

Young American. The volume of Mathews's poems is a *new* book in every sense. "It has, even in the midst of faults neither few nor small, an unequivocal originality and young force and freshness of its own, vigorous in its very rudeness and immaturity, together with a certain earnest spirit of Americanism which comes to us like a breath of new life, of the west wind from our own lofty fast-rooted American mountains, over the stagnant vapors of the East—the East whence blows that sirocco so deadly to American energy." Others may have written more eloquently of some of the topics in this volume (for example, "Emerson in his so called prose lectures, which lack nothing of poetry but the name"), but here there is certainly a strong statement of the "vantage ground in the scale of humanity of the American citizen." Mathews has left "dilletantism [*sic*] and proprieties and 'decencies forever,' and foreign toryism, and English opinion, and the whole wasting brood." He writes of Americans and as an American. The first poem in the volume begins with the beginning of man as a child. "Tennyson would stop to fondle the ringlets, arrange the silken coverlet, and most charmingly compliment the nurse. Mr. Mathews has none of this melodious luxuriousness." Duyckinck and O'Sullivan picked other poems to praise: "The Father" "is as complete a piece of new-world-ism as could well be written." "The Mechanic is in the spirit of Channing." So they proceeded through the poems. The review concluded by asking Mathews to polish the roughness of his verse.[16]

As the *Democratic Review* passed out of Young American hands there were fewer reviews of American poets, but Young Americans still contributed occasionally, and in the later years one essay discussed American poets from the Young American point of view; another essay may be cited to show the end of the Young American regime. The first was a capable, intelligent, and sharply written two-part review of the new poetry of New England. The first part was taken up with a characterization of New England and its people and a discussion of Emerson's poetry. The whole is in sharp contrast to the *Whig's* attitude toward New England and especially toward Emerson. The reviewer began: "From traffic to treason nothing is safe against Yankee versatility. The sons of New-England are omnipresent in every region, whether of space or thought." No matter where you go, you will discover that the New Englander has been there before you, carried "off the best bargains and set up a newspaper." Some are undoubtedly in hell getting ideas for "new patent cooking-stoves and hot air furnaces." New Englanders know particularly well the force of ideas. With an unconquerable love of liberty, a great public spirit, and a love of the family and the home, they will starve, fight, and die for ideas. The majority of the American poets whose names are familiar come of New England stock: Bryant, Dana, Halleck, Whittier, Longfellow, and Willis, to name no others. Their writings all display the love of ideas, "the predominance of intellect"; there is no "rich southern glow" about their writings. And now here are new poets from New England. "First, by right undeniable, we have placed the name of RALPH WALDO EMERSON, whom there is little risk in pronouncing the most original. not only of American poets, but of living writers." As little as the reviewer liked some of his feeble imitators, he liked even less (attention the *Whig Review*) "the whippersnappers and dilettanti who, at safe distance, presume to discharge their pop-guns at the diamond fortress of this man of genius" (much the words used by Lowell in his *Fable* later to describe George Washington Peck of the *Whig*). There followed a good description of an Emerson lecture, the crowd, the delivery and so on.

Emerson, the reviewer continued, is purely New Englander in all his important characteristics: his humor, his "Yankee public spirit," his emphasis upon the intellect at the expense of the "human." His poetry is constructed on a somewhat faulty theory which does not give enough place to "art." But a large portion of the poems he has published stand in need of "no apology or illusion in respect of poetic structure." Since Emerson is not concerned to build a logical philosophical system, it is "impossible for any but a Philistine to criticise Mr. Emerson's philosophy except in the most general manner." The reviewer might wish that some of his religion and philosophy were different: "But what he is, he is; a man of most original, penetrating and beautiful genius. We cannot say that he is a great poet; that title will somehow not apply. The whole tenor of our criticism must, we think, show that such distinction cannot be claimed for him. But this can be said: the whole range of our literature does not furnish his peer in depth of thought, or exhibit such ideals of beauty as can be found in this volume."

The critic then turned to the other volumes of New England poetry, first the poems of William Ellery Channing. Channing has many good qualities: a true human feeling, a love of man as man, a passion for nature and "an appreciation of her analogies," a fancy which sometimes rises to the grander regions of imagination, "a meditative humor," "and an occasional keen skill in the use of words." But he is too careless and slipshod in his work: "Had he been timely pointed to the toils by which the beginner becomes a master, his genius would not now be doing itself such injustice as authorises philistines to sneer at him." William W. Story's volume lacks mainly "concentration and earnestness." "Mr. Story can do better things." Mr. Thomas Buchanan Read's poetry will be the most popular of the group under review: it "is not infected with new ideas." There is some satisfaction in reading a poet who has good digestion, looks only at the outside of things, does not keep one's "brain long on the stretch." "Nature with him is not symbolic." Of Epes Sargent's poetry the reviewer could say little in praise: "To speak plainly, it is not poetry any more than cutting square blocks of marble is sculpture."

Finally the critic summed up. The only poet who is really "new" of those reviewed is Emerson. But even he is not the great American poet we must look for. That poet will not be born in New England: "The great men of this country are to appear beside the mighty rivers and amidst the fruitful fields of the west. Thence too will come to us the poets of immortal name; great, world-embracing souls, who shall weave all things into their strains, and paint as in fire all forms of passion, opening up for man the blessedness of Paradise and the glories of the New Golden Age."[17]

A final review had much to say about the female poets of America and much more about Mr. Griswold and his anthology of female poetry. The review is a *Whig*-type slashing of Griswold and the hapless ladies. It shows also the new regime on the *Demo-cratic,* for it ridiculed the efforts of Margaret Fuller and Mathews to bring an American literature into existence. And it found hardly anything in Griswold's anthology of which it could approve. The critic condemned Griswold roundly because "he leads young innocent damsels astray from the safe paths of prose, and gives us poems to read, remarkable, because of the tender age of the authoress." "Barnum is the man for mammoth children." "Who does not agree with Uncle Toby? When Mr. Shandy told him that the learned Lipsius produced a book soon after his birth, 'Indeed,' quoth he, 'they should have wiped it up, and said no more about it.' "[18]

III

Young America and the *Democratic Review* were no more interested in non-English fiction than they were in foreign poetry. One of the few critical articles in the *Democratic* is a laudatory review, probably by a Young American, of a collection of the tales of Heinrich Zschokke, which was edited by Parke Godwin

and published by Duyckinck. Another article is an interesting
bit of sabotage of the usual tolerant *Democratic* policy in a
review of Eugène Sue's *The Wandering Jew*. Published while
editor O'Sullivan was out of the city, and later apologized for,
the review condemned completely the moral quality of the novel
and through it the whole Fourier movement, which was said to
be seeking the overthrow of marriage and Christianity (Albert
Brisbane was permitted to defend Fourierism in a later number).[19]

Representative opinions of Young America on English novelists may be chosen from among the *Democratic's* reviews.
Generally seeming to share the contemporary high estimate of
Scott and Goldsmith, Young America, nevertheless, preferred
usually to turn to other novelists for review. We have noticed
earlier the praise of Dickens for his democratic fiction on the
occasion of his visit to this country. Later W. A. Jones took the
measure of this reigning favorite of the day and a second favorite,
Bulwer. Dickens, he declared, "is undoubtedly the best living
novelist," but with his undeniable merits he has defects. His
characters run into caricatures: "His muse is riant and oversteps
the modesty of nature." So often compared to Hogarth, he
is, however, closer to Cruikshank. From the high standard of
Scott, Fielding, Smollett, and Irving our praise of Dickens must
be tempered somewhat.

Jones was not so kind to Bulwer. He acknowledged that "no
contemporary writer surpasses Mr. Bulwer, either in pretension
or popularity." But Bulwer is merely a successful literary im-
postor: all his characters are types and spout secondhand sentiment; his philosophy, borrowed from the French, is shallow and
dangerous. His style is "mechanical, elaborate, strained, and tedious." "All his sentences ought to be printed in capitals, for he
tries to be startling in every phrase." He has "tact and great in-
dustry" and is a "very clever compiler of romances." Knowing
all the tricks of bookmaking, he can assume enthusiasm and

write with a "bastard heat." "In fine, he is a skilful literary manufacturer..."

Jones added a summary of the defect common to all modern
fiction. The trouble is that novelists, to be popular, must write
too much and too rapidly, at least a novel a year. They do not
possess enough material for this production: "From nothing,
nothing can come; whence the emptiness and verbiage of most
modern novels, a defect at least equal to the sins of reviewers,
who spin a dozen pages out of what a closer writer could, with
ease, have condensed into a single column."[20]

Finally, we should notice that the *Democratic* gives us what
Carl Van Doren has called a "tolerable article" on Thomas Love
Peacock's *Headlong Hall* and *Nightmare Abbey,* which Duyckinck had just republished in the Library of Choice Reading.
The reviewer was obviously delighted with the books, but he
did not overrate their author's importance: "Coleridge used to
say that Swift was the soul of Rabelais dwelling in a dry place;
substitute Swift for Rabelais, and the remark may be made of
our author. He is at least two removes in literature from the
great original." The critic called *Headlong Hall* "a Spirit of the
Age, secondary only to that of Hazlitt, who has drawn some of
the same characters depicted in this volume." And finally "Headlong Hall and Night-Mare Abbey are books capable of furnish-
ing a great deal of enjoyment to readers of cultivated, speculative
minds; they have the same interest in the skilfully adjusted con-
flicts of the characters, which we take in a game of chess. Victory
hangs on the nicest intellectual balance..."[21]

Somewhat less interested in American fiction than in American poetry, the *Democratic Review* published extended criticisms on Irving, Hawthorne, Cooper, Mathews, Webber, and
Melville, and somewhat less detailed criticisms of others like
Poe, Mrs. Kirkland, Mrs. Farnham, Judge Hall, and Simms.

With sometime Democrat Irving, Young America could not

be so happy as with party-line Bryant, but it did its best by putting him at the head of American fiction, hoping that he would yet turn to works of "higher philosophy and more earnest tone." But Mathews, Hawthorne, and Melville it could praise with less reservation.

E. A. Duyckinck reviewed various books of Mathews in the *New York Review,* the *Whig Review,* and the *Democratic.* In the *New York Review* he hoped that Mathews would be the great American humorist, though he acknowledged that there are marks of haste in the *Motley Book* and that the *Politicians* lacks many of the qualities of the great comedies of Wycherley and Congreve. Reviewing his own edition of *Big Abel and the Little Manhattan* in Wiley & Putnam's series of American books for the *Whig,* Duyckinck complained that no American writer "has been treated less fairly" than Mathews: in this book he shows his faculty of "seeing the picturesque in very common occurrences, and feeling the poetry attached to very ordinary matters." His reviews in the *Democratic* are in the same vein.[22]

As a part of O'Sullivan's program to "manufacture" Hawthorne into a personage, Duyckinck wrote a laudatory review of his works for the *Democratic.* Skillfully enough for his purposes, Duyckinck simply assumed the greatness of Hawthorne:

Nathaniel Hawthorne has passed that period of his literary life in which it is necessary to enter upon a systematic examination of his writings, in the old approved critical style. He is admitted to be a genuine author, simple, natural, and perfect in his peculiar department of writing, and stands upon that vantage ground, where his position being a thing established, one may write of him with freedom, and speak warmly of those points which may appeal most forcibly to his individual taste.

So did the "Silver Pen" glide along, touching upon Hawthorne's perfect style, his light play of fancy, and his deep moral sentiment like that of tempest-stricken Lear (for the latter he analyzed

"Young Goodman Brown" as an example). At the close the critic could only exclaim: "A truly pure, gentle and acceptable man of Genius is NATHANIEL HAWTHORNE!"[23]

The reviewer (probably Duyckinck) of Melville's *Mardi* chided the other critics for failing to see the allegory in *Mardi* and complained that the unique quality of the book had militated against it: "The manner of the book is unique, and like all new things must take the chance of being considered ugly, because it is uncommon." This book is not for those who want a simple romance. "But whoso wishes to see the spirit of philosophy and humanity, love and wisdom showing man to himself as he is, that he may know his evil and folly, and be saved from them, will be reverently thankful for this book." The reviewer could not approve wholly the philosophy of the book: he could not share Melville's "doctrine that this world can be a failure." But he could disregard this difference of opinion: "We have small respect for authors who are wilful, and cannot be advised; but we reverence a man when God's *must* is upon him, and he does his work in his own and other's spite. Portions of Mardi are written with this divine impulse, and they thrill through every fibre of the reader with an electric force."[24]

IV

One of the most significant literary characteristics of the fifteen years before 1850 was the popularity of the essay and the "review" and the all but universal acceptance of such prose forms as an important branch of "literature." Young American critics often pointed out that the two types of popular literature of the day were the novel and the review (or essay). And since Young Americans did perhaps more than their share of the reviewing of this popular form, the comparatively brief account which follows should not be taken to indicate the relative space they devoted to such forms in the *Democratic Review* or elsewhere.

Something of the quantity of criticism on the essay and the related prose forms in the *Democratic Review* may be indicated by the sheer bulk of a partial list of the foreign writers (English and Continental) who were given extended attention: Carlyle, Schiller, Macaulay, Fanny Burney, Swift, Bolingbroke, Addison, Hazlitt, Jeffrey, Defoe, Johnson, Burke, Junius, Sir Thomas Browne, Steele, Pope, Lady Mary Montague, Gray, Cowper, Taylor, Barrow, Tillotson, South, Berkeley, Sterne, and Lamb.

Young America, chiefly through W. A. Jones, concentrated on three kinds of writers for its reviews of foreign prose writers, all of which are fully represented in the *Democratic Review*. Democratic politicians and publicists could have learned much from the first type of review: the historical surveys of political writers. Since we have already noticed in detail what Jones had to say about the general qualities of good political writing we need only suggest something of his estimate of particular writers. He declared Swift superior to Bolingbroke, called Defoe Addison in homespun. Addison's *Freeholder* is the *Spectator* turned politician: "There is the same fine sense and elegant humor, the same elevation of sentiment and satiric wit, the same classicality and finished style." Despite Dr. Johnson's Tory politics Jones could but respect him. Burke had "an eloquence and brilliancy unsurpassed in political oratory and political writing." Junius was Burke cut down, a refined gentleman with a cutting sneer and polished sarcasm.[25]

A second major interest was in the prose of "The Old English Pulpit," which we have also already noticed in some detail. Jeremy Taylor was obviously Jones's favorite, as the usual form of greatest praise—calling him a poet—makes clear: "A poet should be the critic of Jeremy Taylor, for he was one himself ..." But Robert South, Barrow, Donne, Sherlock, and others shared in his praise.[26]

The recent review writers of England and the Edinburgh

school of critics constitute a third Young American interest. As might be expected, they, through Jones, judged Macaulay and Carlyle the best contemporary review writers in England. "Macaulay, the Edinburgh reviewer, is, probably the most brilliant writer of English prose now living, the last remaining member of that glorious band of wits, critics and fine thinkers, who constituted the force of the Edinburgh in its prime—Jeffrey, Macintosh [*sic*], Hazlitt, Brougham, Carlyle, Stephens [*sic*], and himself ..." Macaulay, however, is not a critic, nor an original judge, nor a lecturer, "but that rare union of critic and miscellaneous writer—a critical essayist." Carlyle, said Jones, is the opposite of Macaulay on almost every score. Though he agreed with Carlyle's criticism of society, Jones could not agree with Carlyle's prescription for its ills: "Carlyle's practical suggestions of education, emigration, and the like, are not sufficient. They are highly useful, but much more is needed ..." *Sartor Resartus* is his master work: "It is close, ingenious, profound, and earnest; full of a deep satirical humor that, like all true humor, conceals deep thought and feeling ..." Yet Carlyle is not a "pure, original genius" but a man of "consummate talent."[27]

In criticizing the Edinburgh school of critics, Jones took a side glance at the unfortunate Gifford and the London *Quarterly*. Of Gifford, "This old crab-apple was a cobbler to the *very last*— a word-catcher, a dove-tailer and joiner of sentences, a literary mechanic." Jones followed Gifford with a rhapsodic tribute to Hazlitt, "the first of the regular critics in this nineteenth century." He wrote of his "wide grasp" and "manly cast of intellect," his freshness, "creative talent and fine ingenuity," his "analytic judgment" and "poetic fancy."

As a descriptive writer, in his best passages he ranks with Burke and Rousseau, in delineation of sentiment, and in a rich rhetorical vein, he has whole pages worthy of Taylor or Lord Bacon. There is nothing in Macaulay, for profound gorgeous declamation, superior to the character of Coleridge, or of Milton, or of Burke ... In pure criticism, who has done so much for the novelists, the essayists, writers of comedy; for the old dramatists and elder poets? Lamb's fine notes are mere notes—Coleridge's improvised criticisms are merely fragmentary, while if Hazlitt has borrowed their opinions in some cases, he has made much more of them than they could have done themselves.

Jones explained the reasons for Hazlitt's relative unpopularity, but concluded that "the best critics now living in England and this country belong, emphatically, to the school of Hazlitt." In this judgment Young America again differed with the *Whig* reviewers: E. P. Whipple made a similar claim for conservative Coleridge, when he said that "all the most popular critics of the day, more or less follow his mode of judgment and investigation."[28]

Jones also dealt with the other Edinburgh reviewers. Sir James Mackintosh was praised as "a critic of philosophical systems, especially in ethics and politics." Lord Brougham was thought more accomplished as an active reformer than as a speculative reformer. Jeffrey, given more space than any of the group except Hazlitt, was defended from the calumny so often heaped upon him. His temperament, Jones said, did not fit him to be a critic of poetry: his "egregious mistakes" in judgment grew out of a faulty French and eighteenth-century system of criticism to which he adhered, not out of a "malicious perversion of the truth" or a "mean desire to depreciate genius." We must remember, too, his later regard for the poetry of Keats. Of prose he is a good critic; "With his clear, shrewd, professional eye he detects, at once, sophisms, absurdities, quackeries, of all sorts."[29]

As the economic forces directed toward writers from the conditions of publishing in America turned American authors to lecturing and essay writing for the magazines and reviews, Young American critics kept up with the burgeoning new form in many reviews in the *Democratic*. Two American essayists and lecturers were the especial heroes of Young America and the *Democratic Review.*

If *Arcturus,* as Lowell remarked, was as transcendental as New York could be, the *Democratic Review* and the Young Americans writing for it were as transcendental as Democrats could be. While the critics in the Whig *New York Review* and the *Whig Review* were ridiculing, scolding, vilifying Emerson, Jones and other critics in *Arcturus* and the *Democratic Review* were generally praising him. Jones's epigrammatic remarks on Emerson and the transcendentalists represent the attitude of the liberal critics of Young America.

After tracing Emerson's thought back to Carlyle and the Germans, Jones characterized the transcendentalists as a school of thinkers which holds no very precise doctrines. Independent in their opinions, they "unite to differ." "Referring everything to the individual soul, they must entertain within themselves a contrariety of belief, a mixture of systems. They are now shrewd and practical, again absurd and visionary, at last high and spiritual." They are "at once mystical, aphoristic, oracular." By dwelling on a narrow range of topics—topics relating to progress, insight, and the individual soul—they narrow their whole thought. "Their favorite method of composition seems to be transposition, involution, a conciseness approaching to obscurity, and sometimes actually obscuring the thought." Unfortunately their oracles are not always true: "There are lying prophets among them." As, in Jones's opinion, the best of the group, Emerson deserved the fullest attention.

He described Emerson's fancy as the scholar's fancy: "elaborate, quaint, artificial; a little exaggerated, slightly fantastical; caught, perhaps, from foreign sources; a revival probably of Plato, of the poetic Neo-Platonists, strangely mingled with the dreams of Swedenborg, the reveries of the Kantian philosophy, and the noble aspirations of Goethe." Emerson should be censured for the want of continuity in his style, but he is to be commended for the "pointed sentences, shrewd remarks and occasional fullness of rich declamation." *Nature* he singled out for particular attention, calling it "an essay descriptive, aesthetical, moral, psychological and prophetic. It is full of matter, pithy, shrewd, and often eloquent." Certain descriptions in it are examples of "what description ought to be—the actual landscape, with a coloring of reflection; in a word, a sentimental picture." All in all, Jones concluded, Emerson is "in the first rank of the thinkers of this country."[30]

Against this Young American opinion of Emerson the conservatives opposed themselves vigorously. The *New York Review* two years before Jones's essay had professed to find it hard to describe its feelings in reading Emerson: "The tear dropped over prostituted beauty approaches nearer to the sensation, where all that is beautiful and lovely in taste and talent is made ... the destroyer of man's fairest hopes of happiness here and hereafter." A year after Jones's essay the *Whig* objected to the coterie which had developed around Emerson, summarized Emerson's "Experience" as an example of his writing, and remarked that the "partial and inadequate character" of his *"Human Pantheism"* is manifest, "and its errors expose themselves." Two years later the *Whig* became offensively personal in its objections to Emerson. George Gilfillan had described the light in Emerson's face when he speaks; R. H. Bacon commented: "Mr. Emerson's features, when excited, light up a little; just as does the face of even an idiot when a transient glow of momentary intelligence flashes across it."[31]

The second hero of Young America is perhaps more surprising. From 1839 to 1843 the *Democratic Review* contained five articles on William Ellery Channing. The first praised the noble character of Channing and reviewed *Self-Culture:* it is the best of his writings, for it is "thoroughly embued with that spirit of elevated democracy and expansive philanthropy that have long characterized its author." The next commended his democratic philosophy (though he is not really partisan, a later review said, he is Locofoco in his democracy). The following one said more about his style. He is "one of the most pure and elegant of the living masters of the language." His style has a "limpid clearness," "a chaste but severe beauty," and a "vigorous Anglo-Saxon force and energy" when necessary. The final two essays, one by George Bancroft, were tributes to him upon his death.[32]

Other criticisms of American prose writers follow much this pattern; praise is most evident for political liberals like Paine, Leggett, and Bryant, and for those followers of Emerson who, "lacking utterly all basis of good sense," are, according to the *Whig Review,* "in our literature the exact counterpart of the Democratic party in our politics." The tone of the criticism of both groups may be suggested by Jones's remarks on the radical political writing of sometime transcendentalist Orestes Brownson (a contributor to the *Democratic*). Brownson's style is "full of vigor and earnestness, but to the last degree copious, and running over into diffuseness." Yet it is never "vague and unmeaning, however prolix and tiresome." His "celebrated pamphlet" on property and inheritance "is not much inferior to the best political writing of Hazlitt, full of personal feeling and a certain colloquial energy"—this of an author whose writings caused one Whig journal to regret "that the revisers of our criminal code, should not have preserved the salutary discipline of the pillory and whipping-post."[33]

v

This account has shown that Young America's critical judgments of specific authors were usually consistent with its general, more abstract religious, political, social, and literary theories. In its most representative journal Young America distributed critical awards in a way which shows especially clearly its liberal political prejudices, which are, however, though more open and candid, no more marked than the prejudices of the conservative opposition.

That Young America's social and political outlook was aggressively liberal and American goes far toward explaining the group's most distinctive critical judgments: its approving reviews of eighteenth-century English poets and social thinkers and of new, unconventional American writers. The Democracy of the country had long been accustomed to look to the Enlightenment for inspiration; critics devoted to the promotion of a new political and social order readily accepted writers who dealt with new subjects in a new manner. Young America did not always avoid the pitfalls that its tolerance opened before it; taking as its task the encouragement of even mediocrity in American literature, it sometimes fell into an easy literary democracy which approved of anything written by an American or, at least, by an American Democrat. Fortunately for the future reputation of its critical estimates, most contemporary American writers of importance were Democrats or sympathetic toward the aims of the party. The Locofoco politico-literary system led to the approval of such new writers as Emerson, Hawthorne, Melville, and the "folk" humorists, and Young America's control of important publishing mediums and its understanding of the new system of commercial patronage made its encouragement practical as well as critical.

In their efforts to support new and experimental writing of every sort, but particularly new democratic and liberal writing, Young America had opposition at every step. In the closing lines of *A Fable for Critics,* James Russell Lowell characterized that opposition and named a representative critic of the conservative school.

'Tis delightful to see, when a man comes along
Who has anything in him peculiar and strong,
Every cockboat that swims clear its fierce (pop) gun-deck at him,
And make as he passes its ludicrous Peck at him . . .

George Washington Peck was explicit in his conservatism and in speaking of its effect on his criticism. Reviewing Melville in the *Whig Review,* he wrote: "We have felt obliged, as a conservative in literature . . . to say many severe things—the more severe, because they are against the tone and spirit of the book, and therefore apply more directly to its author." Peck always spoke highly of the better days when "the 'one progressive principle,' Democracy," was not in the ascendant. Today "authors less and less address themselves to a judicious few, and more and more to an unreflecting many"—that is, we see too much poetry for the people, literature for the million. "There are demagogues in letters as in politics." The essence of literary, political, and religious conservatism is concentrated in Peck's querulous complaint about the productions of Young America, transcendentalists, and writers like George Sand whom the group often championed: "If these writers would only leave us alone in our simple religious faith, in our common views of God, ourselves, and the world . . . But they *muddle the mind,* and make the voice of reason and conscience 'an uncertain sound.' " And these radicals are so noisy in their claims: "It is the instinct of a radical, no less in philosophy and letters than in politics, to be noisy."[34]

To which, as we have seen, Young America answered again and again, sometimes quite noisily, as Melville did in reviewing Democrat Hawthorne in Young American Duyckinck's *Literary World:* "But what sort of a belief is this for an American, a man who is bound to carry republican progressiveness into Literature as well as into Life?"[35]

Chapter VI

CONCLUSION

B Y 1850 the Young Americans were beginning to go their separate ways. The reforming Democratic Party of the 'thirties and 'forties was disintegrating under the impact of the slavery question: there was no longer a center around which Young America could rally. The *Democratic Review* had passed into the hands of a conservative Democrat and was later to be guided by George N. Sanders, a Young American of a different sort. John L. O'Sullivan was forcing Manifest Destiny's hand by filibustering to Cuba (on a ship loaded with a printing press and musical instruments as well as arms, so that the Cubans could be civilized as soon as they were subdued by their destiny), and was later shocking John Bigelow by supporting the South in the Civil War (as did his friend Hawthorne). Cornelius Mathews was continuing his quarrelsome independence. William A. Jones in 1851 became Librarian of Columbia College and ceased writing criticism. And E. A. Duyckinck, the final key member of Young America, was principally concerned with editing the *Literary World,* in which the Locofoco politico-literary system was sputtering out as the fuel of the reforming impulse was gradually withdrawn.

Added to the decline of liberalism as a major factor in turning Young America in other directions was the decline of New York as a publishing center. Before mid-century, most American literature was published in New York or Philadelphia—and somewhat more in New York than in Philadelphia. Much of even the flowering of New England, as William Charvat has shown, went on in New York and Philadelphia. But by mid-century James T. Fields and other Boston book publishers and promoters were beginning to carry literature to Boston or keep it there;[1] Duyckinck, Putnam, and other New York publishers were losing the battle to make New York the center of American literature. New York and some of the Young Americans like Duyckinck, Godwin, and now Melville, continued the fight in the *Literary World* and later in *Putnam's Monthly*. But Boston's complete triumph is patly symbolized by two events in 1857: the end of *Putnam's Monthly* in New York, and the start of the *Atlantic Monthly* in Boston.

But even in 1850 Oliver Wendell Holmes, that perfect exponent of the Hub of the Universe, was not too wide of the mark in ridiculing the pretensions of New York Young Americans. Holmes had spent a few days in the Berkshires with, among others, Hawthorne, Melville, J. T. Headley, Duyckinck, Mathews, and James T. Fields, during which, as we have noticed earlier, Melville had attacked him for speaking against Young American positions. A week later, in a poem delivered before Phi Beta Kappa at Yale, in a passage which he later left out of his collected editions, he attacked certain critics:

> The pseudo-critic-editorial race
> Owns no allegiance but the law of place;
> Each to his region sticks through thick and thin,
> Stiff as a beetle spiked upon a pin.
> Plant him in Boston, and his sheet he fills
> With all the slipslop of his threefold hills ...

But it is not mainly Boston critics that he ridicules:

> But Hudson's banks, with more congenial skies,
> Swells the small creature to alarming size;

the critic begins to hiss "provincial" and "metropolis":

> He cry "provincial" with imperious brow!
> The half-bred rogue, that groomed his mother's cow!

A "third-rate college" (Duyckinck and Mathews attended Columbia) shaped him into a scholar's ape, who could puff "titanic

[1] For notes to chapter vi see page 141.

pygmies" into wide renown—for miles along Harlem road. "God bless Manhattan!"

> Yet not too rashly let her think to bind
> Beneath her circlet all the nation's mind;

for doubtless some "poison lurks in her commercial air" to kill genius prematurely. But let her not give up hope:

> Some future day may see her rise sublime
> Above her counters,—only give her time!

When our first soldiers hang their swords there, our first statesmen "take the Broadway track," our first historians follow them, our first painters fill her walls,

> When our first Poets flock from farthest scenes
> To take in hand her pictured Magazines;
> When our first Scholars are content to dwell
> Where their own printers teach them how to spell;
> When world-known Science crowds toward her gates,
> Then shall the children of our hundred States
> Hail her a true Metropolis of men,
> The nation's centre. Then, and not till then!

Let Mathews and Duyckinck cry out as angrily as they pleased at this—as they did in the *Literary World,*—Holmes was correct: in 1850 the day of New York's supremacy in literature and publishing, at least, was in the past and in the future.[2]

But the Young Americans of New York—all still only in their thirties—could in 1850 look back on certain solid achievements as literary critics. They had added new dimensions to American literary criticism.

In the first place no critics before them had so consistently drawn upon American democratic liberalism—political, social, and religious—as a standard for judging literature. The year 1837, which saw the publication of Emerson's *American Scholar* and the founding of the *Democratic Review,* marks an important date in the movement toward maturity and independence in American literature.

Even the absurdities and failures of Young America in espousing a democratic literature are—apart from their historical significance—instructive: the hazards of a literature and a criticism tied closely to politics and a political party are here laid bare—where are the Jacksonians, the Marxists, the New Dealers of yesteryear? The answer must be that those who are more "politico" than "literary" live on only in the cold storage of historian's minds and books. But what of those who are "literary" first, political only secondarily? The history of Young America suggests a tentative answer to this question also. Surely it must be granted that their following of the reform party, the party of the "people," the party devoted to the "new," helped them to see the realities of the new democratic or commercial system of patronage and to assist American authors in adjusting to it; to recognize and approve such new writers as Emerson, Hawthorne, and Melville; to develop a democratic theory of literature that had its culmination in an even more experimental writer, Walt Whitman, poet of and for the people, "Homer of the mass"; to see the literary possibilities in the realistic humor of the American "people," even of the Western "life on the Mississippi" of Mark Twain.

And this answer points to a second historical significance of the literary criticism of Young America. It has not been the purpose of this account to show the influence of Young American ideas on major American writers, but certain influences have been suggested, and that there were many others cannot be doubted. From Christopher Pearse Cranch and the young William Ellery Channing to Thoreau and Emerson the transcendentalists knew and were writing for the *Democratic Review*. Emerson's letters, his essays on "The Poet" and "The Young American," show especially clearly his awareness of their work.

Hawthorne, Whittier, Lowell, and Bryant were prolific contributors to the *Democratic* and must have known Young American criticism from it, if from no other source. Even Poe, as we have seen, while disagreeing with Young America on some points, commended the high quality of *Arcturus* and the *Democratic Review*—disagreement can be stimulating. And Melville and Simms were closer to Young America than any of the foregoing.

But of all the writers it is quite obvious that Walt Whitman must have learned the most from Young America. In the years when Young America flourished, Whitman was, of course, a Democratic journalist who contributed stories (stories "à la Hawthorne," according to Lowell) to the *Democratic Review* and followed its monthly numbers, clipping out some articles which are still in his papers. Writing in the Brooklyn *Daily Times* in 1858, he described somewhat nostalgically the *Democratic* of the 'forties as "a monthly magazine of a profounder quality of talent than any since"; it "was largely impressing the public, especially the young men"; "its corps of writers were all enthusiasts—believers in 'a good time coming.' "[3] Whitman, one of "its corps of writers," remained an "enthusiast" for precisely those ideas that are most characteristic of Young America: democracy, America's destiny, as much of transcendentalism as a Democratic son of Manhattan could swallow, and the duty of the American poet, heedless of the canons of the "mechanical critics" of the aristocratic past, to observe the "people" and express the progressive "spirit of the age." That Whitman was so lonely a voice in 1855 was due partly to the fact that the *Democratic Review* and Young America had been dispersed by that time. Yet, even in the full flush of its enthusiasm, Young America, like Emerson, might have shuddered somewhat at seeing a poet take its ideas seriously; *Leaves of Grass* was more disturbing, to put it mildly, than Cornelius Mathews's *Poems on Man, in His Various Aspects under the American Republic*.

Of other achievements to which Young America could look back in 1850, we may remind ourselves of only a few. Some of the group, along with a few other contemporary critics, had demonstrated that the United States could support (somewhat precariously) professional literary critics. It was no longer true in America that literary criticism was written as an avocation by a "homogeneous upper class" in society which reflected its social and economic bias.[4] Most Young Americans and many other critics of the time were not members of an upper class, but of a separate group in society: the intelligentsia, the literati, or the free intellectuals. They were members of a group in society who make their livings from their intellect or whose primary interests are in intellectual affairs, and who choose their political and social views by some process which is not an automatic rationalization for their social and economic status in the community. E. A. Duyckinck, a man of means and high in the society of New York, could choose the Movement party; George Washington Peck and Henry Norman Hudson, farm boys from New England, could become conservative supporters of the Establishment party. Moreover, the relatively high quality of some of the Young American criticism reflects the new status of the critic: as C. A. Bristed observed in 1848 in *Blackwood's,* after citing the *Democratic Review,* "if good critics are well paid, it will be worth men's while to study to become good critics."[5]

Ironically for critics so clamorously American, another service of Young America was to help in bringing the liberal strains of English "Romanticism" and the newer stimulation of Utilitarianism to America. They helped to show Americans that Hazlitt, Shelley, Bentham, and Mill, as well as Coleridge and Wordsworth, had something to say to them. But Young America, it should be noted, though its periodicals might sometimes look like the Benthamite *Westminster Review,* and though it might delight in Peacock's fiction, usually tended to agree with Shelley that the culture of the imagination had a "higher" usefulness that should not be denied.

Historically important and still relevant is a final lesson that we may read in Young America: Young America made its basic social, political, and literary assumptions explicit. The resulting candor and self-awareness stimulated a considerable segment of the literary and intellectual life of the country—extending its influence even to the conservatives. Emerson's observation, with which we began, needs little qualification: though there may be gradations between them, in intellectual and social affairs "there *are* always two parties, the party of the Past and the party of the Future; the Establishment and the Movement." And the intellectual—perhaps most of all the critic and historian—works best when he is aware of this fact, as was Young America. Young America did not succeed often in stimulating what Poe called the "criticism of the conservatives," the criticism "of the cultivated old clergymen of the *North American Review*," who opened "their mouths with proper caution" to "sigh forth the word '*Repose*'"; but in New York it was more successful. The conservative gentility of New York was forced more and more to declare itself, to bring its assumptions up for review, to face issues: "its Serene Highness," as the *Democratic Review* called it, the *New York Review* gave way to the *Whig Review*, which frankly admitted its political and social assumptions and with considerable candor debated issues with the Democrats and Young America. The cold bloods of American literary critics were not again so warmed and quickened until after the Civil War, when William Dean Howells in the new American literary center began forcing other issues.

NOTES, BIBLIOGRAPHY, AND INDEX

NOTES TO CHAPTER I

POLITICS, MAGAZINES, AND PUBLISHING

(Pages 1-16)

[1] "Historic Notes of Life and Letters in New England," *Complete Works of Ralph Waldo Emerson*, X, 325.

[2] "The New York Press," *New-York Mirror*, III, 46 (October 25, 1845).

[3] William Trimble, "The Social Philosophy of the Loco-Foco Democracy," *American Journal of Sociology*, XXVI, 709 (May, 1921). For further information on the Loco-focos, see this article and another by Trimble, "Diverging Tendencies in New York Democracy in the Period of the Loco-focos," *American Historical Review*, XXIV, 396–421 (April, 1919).

[4] Trimble, "Social Philosophy," p. 710.

[5] Quoted in A. M. Schlesinger, Jr., *The Age of Jackson*, p. 313.

[6] "The War of the Five Campaigns," *Democratic Review*, VII, 486 (June, 1840). For details of this "counter-reformation," see "The Whig Counter-Reformation," and "1840," in Schlesinger, *Jackson*, pp. 267–305.

[7] "Prospectus of the American Review," *Whig Review*, II, second page of cover (August, 1845); "Introductory," *Whig Review*, I, 1 (January, 1845).

[8] Letter of J. L. O'Sullivan to R. W. Griswold, September 8, 1842, *Passages from the Correspondence and Other Papers of Rufus W. Griswold*, p. 123; "Introduction," *Democratic Review*, I, 13 (October, 1837).

[9] Letter of J. L. O'Sullivan to R. W. Griswold, September 8, 1842, Griswold, *Passages*, p. 123; Schlesinger, *Jackson*, pp. 371–372; Adams's mention of Langtree's visit, October 21, 1837, *Memoirs of John Quincy Adams*, IX, 416.

[10] William Gilmore Simms congratulated Duyckinck on his "accession" to the literary helm of the *Democratic* in an unpublished letter, April 10, 1845, in the Duyckinck papers at the New York Public Library; unpublished letter of J. L. O'Sullivan, July 6, 1845, in the same collection.

[11] "The Magazines," *Broadway Journal*, I, 93 (February 18, 1845); *Democratic Review*, VII, iii (1840); Schlesinger, *Jackson*, p. 373; unpublished letter of J. L. O'Sullivan to E. A. Duyckinck, July 6, 1845, in the Duyckinck papers at the New York Public Library; "The Periodical Literature of America," *Blackwood's Magazine*, LXIII, 111 (January, 1848).

[12] Julian Hawthorne, *Nathaniel Hawthorne and His Wife*, I, 159; letter of J. L. O'Sullivan to John Bigelow, July 22, 1842, John Bigelow, *Retrospections of an Active Life*, I, 64; F. B. Sanborn, *Hawthorne and His Friends*, p. 31; letter of H. D. Thoreau to his mother, October 1, 1843, *Familiar Letters of Henry David Thoreau*, p. 129.

[13] "Literary Phenomena," *Whig Review*, IV, 408 (October, 1846).

[14] "Literary Physicians," *Democratic Review*, XIII, 595 (December, 1843).

[15] Letter of September 8, 1843, "The Emerson-Thoreau Correspondence," *Atlantic Monthly*, LXIX, 593 (May, 1892).

[16] Letter to R. W. Emerson, August 7, 1843, *Familiar Letters*, pp. 121–122; letter to his mother, August 6, 1843, *ibid.*, p. 119; letter to R. W. Emerson, September 14, 1843, "The Emerson-Thoreau Correspondence," *Atlantic Monthly*, LXIX, 593–594 (May, 1892).

[17] Letter to George W. Greene, November, 1840, "Letters of George W. Sumner, 1837–1844," *Proceedings of the Massachusetts Historical Society*, XLVI, 359–360 (March, 1913).

[18] Julian Hawthorne, *Hawthorne and His Wife,* I, 284–285.

[19] Letter to G. B. Loring, March 15, 1841, *Letters of James Russell Lowell,* I, 62.

[20] "Capital Punishment," Brooklyn *Daily Times,* May 22, 1858, in *Uncollected Poetry and Prose of Walt Whitman,* II, 15; [E. A. Poe] "Our Magazine Literature," *New World,* VI, 302 (March 11, 1843); George Parsons Lathrop, *A Study of Hawthorne,* p. 199; F. L. Mott, *A History of American Magazines,* I, 683.

[21] J. D. W[helpley]., "Oliver Goldsmith," *Whig Review,* X, 498 (November, 1849).

[22] For the industrialization of printing and New York's leadership in publishing, see Lawrence C. Wroth, "Book Production and Distribution from the Beginning to the War Between the States," in Hellmut Lehmann-Haupt, *The Book in America,* pp. 63–64, 100; J. Henry Harper, *The House of Harper: A Century of Publishing in Franklin Square,* p. 47; and William Charvat, "James T. Fields and the Beginnings of Book Promotion, 1840–1855," *Huntington Library Quarterly,* VIII, 76 (November, 1944).

[23] For the story of cheap books and best sellers, see Wroth, "Book Production," p. 101; S. G. Goodrich, *Recollections of a Lifetime,* II, 383; Harper, *House of Harper,* pp. 75–77; F. L. Mott, *Golden Multitudes: The Story of Best Sellers in the United States,* p. 77 and the whole chapter " 'The Great Revolution in Publishing,' " pp. 76–79; H. C. Carey, *Letters on International Copyright;* G. P. Putnam, *American Facts,* p. 80; O. A. Roorbach, *Bibliotheca Americana.* Writers often contrast the prices of books in England and in the United States. *Jane Eyre,* for example, was sold at $7.50 in England and at 25 cents in America (Carey, *Letters,* p. 57)

[24] "English and American Literature," *Democratic Review,* XXII, 208 (March, 1848).

[25] "The Yucatan Ruins," *ibid.,* XII, 491 (May, 1843).

[26] Henry Walcott Boynton (*Annals of American Bookselling, 1638–1850,* p. 185) says that the prosperity of Harpers "was largely founded on the lack of an international copyright law"; Wroth, "Book Production," p. 95. The whole copyright question is another example of how literary matters became intermeshed with political arguments in this period. International copyright amounted to a protective tariff. For this and other reasons it was hard for a Democrat to advocate what amounted to a tariff on books in order to encourage home manufacture; those, like Bryant, who did had to show that the justice of the copyright law was based on other grounds than the protective system.

[27] "Literary Prospects of 1845," *Whig Review,* I, 148–149 (February, 1845).

[28] "Contemporary Poetry Criticism," *New Republic,* CV, 88 (July 21, 1941). The contemporary reputation of many nineteenth-century critics may be largely accounted for on the basis of their being able to sell books. E. P. Whipple liked almost everything, or, if he did not like a book, he did not write about it. He probably had no trouble in finding a publisher for his collected essays and in thus achieving a form of distinction not reached by many critics. Poe's difficulties in publishing may have been partly occasioned by his propensity to slashing reviews.

[29] "On Writing for the Magazines," *Democratic Review,* XVI, 457 (May, 1845).

[30] Unpublished letters of E. A. Duyckinck to W. A. Jones, Monday, February 16, 1846, and J. T. Headley to Duyckinck, in the Duyckinck papers at the New York Public Library.

[31] Henry Norman Hudson, "Festus," *Whig Review,* V, 43–45 (January, 1847); [W. A. Jones] "The Culture of the Imagination," *Arcturus,* I, 236–243 (March, 1841).

NOTES TO CHAPTER II

THE YOUNG AMERICANS

(Pages 17–38)

[1] This information is taken from unpublished manuscripts in the Duyckinck papers at the New York Public Library, and, unless otherwise indicated, letters referred to hereafter are to be found in that collection: letter of Cornelius Mathews to E. A. Duyckinck, Friday afternoon, no date; letter from "a party of Young Ladies."

[2] Letter of George L. Duyckinck to W. A. Jones, January 11, 1839; "The Literati of New York City," *Complete Works of Edgar Allan Poe*, XV, 59.

[3] *Pathfinder*, I, 30 (March 4, 1843); letter of Parke Godwin to E. A. Duyckinck, December 6, [1844 ?]; for William Leggett's career, see Richard Hofstadter, "William Leggett, Spokesman of Jacksonian Democracy," *Political Science Quarterly*, LVIII, 581–594 (December, 1943), and Page S. Procter, Jr., "William Leggett (1801–1839): Journalist and Literator," *Papers of the Bibliographical Society of America*, XLIV, 239–253 (Third Quarter, 1950).

[4] " 'Young America,' " *American Historical Review*, XXXII, 34–55 (October, 1926). For an excellent study of one European group, see Georg Brandes, *Main Currents in Nineteenth Century Literature*, Vol. VI: *Young Germany*.

[5] See Merle Curti, "George N. Sanders—American Patriot of the Fifties," *South Atlantic Quarterly*, XXVII, 79–87 (January, 1928).

[6] *Democratic Review*, XXX, 396–397 (May, 1852). *see n* ꞏtests *Literary Wise-men of Gotham*

[7] Quoted in Nathaniel Hawthorne, *American Notebooks*, pp. 288–289. O'Sullivan had only temporarily given up the editorship of the review.

[8] Letter to Margaret Fuller, February 12, 1843, *Letters of Ralph Waldo Emerson*, III, 146–147.

[9] The undated manuscript is in the Duyckinck papers at the New York Public Library.

[10] *John-Donkey*, I, 222 (April 1, 1848).

[11] Undated letter, but the articles indicate September, 1843.

[12] Poe, "Literati," *Complete Works*, XV, 58.

[13] For the Home Library, see George T. Goodspeed, "The Home Library," *Papers of the Bibliographical Society of America*, XLII, 110–118 (Second Quarter, 1948).

[14] "The Library of Choice Reading," *Democratic Review*, XX, 236–239 (March, 1847).

[15] Emerson, *Letters*, III, 297.

[16] Letters of R. H. Dana to E. A. Duyckinck, April 18, 1845, and April 7, 1847; Emerson, *Letters*, III, 384.

[17] Emerson, *Letters*, III, 397

[18] "The Editor's Table," *Knickerbocker*, XXVIII, 451 (November, 1846); for Young America's opinion of the *North American*, see W. A. Jones's statement: "The defect of the North American . . . has been its *literary toryism*, . . . its apparent dislike of innovation and new writers" ("Criticism in America," *Democratic Review*, XV, 244 [September, 1844]).

[19] Letter to George L. Duyckinck. Other letters of Henry William Herbert and R. H. Dana to E. A. Duyckinck discuss the quarrel. The connection with a publishing house had the obvious effect on Duyckinck's criticism: as we have seen, he puffed the authors that he was publishing. But the important thing to notice is that he chose to publish and puff many excellent writers.

[20] Jones ("Criticism in America," p. 245) indicates his financial position: "This fine writer requires but the stimulus of necessity, of which, unfortunately for us, though happily for him, he is free."

[21] Samuel Osgood, *Evert Augustus Duyckinck, His Life, Writings, and Influence*, pp. 13–14; entry for March 17, 1839, in an unpublished diary in the Duyckinck papers at the New York Public Library.

[22] Letter of Auld to George L. Duyckinck and William Allen Butler [1848 ?].

[23] Letter to W. A. Jones, Friday evening, July 28, 1848.

[24] Letters of Francis Bowen to E. A. Duyckinck, December 31, 1842; January 10, 1843; January 27, 1843; February 2, 1843.

[25] E. A. Duyckinck to W. A. Jones, no date.

[26] "American Humor," *Democratic Review*, XVII, 217 (September, 1845). Jones added: "Already he has done more for American and (for some later and old) English authors than any other one writer in the country."

[27] *Herman Melville, Representative Selections*, p. xxiii.

[28] "Several Days in Berkshire," *Literary World*, VII, 166 (August 31, 1850).

[29] *Duyckinck*, p. 5.

[30] "Sketches of American Prose Writers. No. 1. William A. Jones," *Broadway Journal*, I, 28 (January 11, 1845); "Horne's New Spirit of the Age," *Democratic Review*, XV, 49 (July, 1844).

[31] *Memorial of the Late Honorable David S. Jones*, pp. 26–27, 94.

[32] *Ibid.*, p. 94.

[33] "The Democratic Review," *Broadway Journal*, II, 168–169 (September 20, 1845); "About Critics and Criticism," *Complete Works*, XIII, 193. The earlier comment on Jones was provoked by Jones's declaration that only trash had appeared in *Graham's* and *Godey's*.

[34] "The New York Press," *New-York Mirror*, III, 46 (October 25, 1845).

[35] See Pratt's "The Origin of 'Manifest Destiny,' " *American Historical Review*, XXXII, 795–798 (July, 1927); "John L. O'Sullivan and Manifest Destiny," *New York History*, XIV, 214–234 (July, 1933); and his article on O'Sullivan in the *Dictionary of American Biography*.

[36] *Julian Hawthorne and His Wife*, I, 160; Longfellow's opinion, quoted earlier, is in Hawthorne, *American Notebooks*, pp. 288–289; letter of Poe to F. W. Thomas, September 12, 1842, *Letters of Edgar Allan Poe*, I, 211; letter of Thoreau to Emerson, January 24, 1843, *Familiar Letters*, pp. 59–60; Harold P. Miller, "Hawthorne Surveys His Contemporaries," *American Literature*, XII, 230 (May, 1940).

[37] See Merle Curti, "The Reputation of America Overseas (1776–1860)," *American Quarterly*, I, 81–82 (Spring, 1949).

[38] "Notes about Men of Note," *Aristidean*, I, 154–155 (April, 1845).

[39] Letter of February 9, 1846.

[40] Letters of July 15, 1845; November 13, 1845.

[41] Entry for January 13, 1843, in an unpublished diary in the Duyckinck papers at the New York Public Library; letter of August, 1843, "Letters of James Russell Lowell, 1843–54," *Bulletin of the New York Public Library*, IV, 340 (October, 1900).

[42] Mathews, "Several Days in Berkshire," p. 166; letter of E. A. Duyckinck, August 6, 1850, in Luther Stearns Mansfield, "Glimpses of Herman Melville's Life in Pittsfield, 1850–1851," *American Literature*, IX, 30 (March, 1937); "Hawthorne and His Mosses," *Literary World*, VII, 125–127; 145–147 (August 17 and 24, 1850).

[43] Taylor, Halleck, and Jones quoted in Nelson Frederick Adkins, *Fitz-Greene Halleck: An Early Knickerbocker Wit and Poet*, pp. 286, 289, 424, 414; Dana's letter to Jones quoted in James Grant Wilson, *The Life and Letters of Fitz-Greene Halleck*, p.

542; letters of Dana to Duyckinck, April 7, 1847; December 18, 1847; January 20, 1848; January 25, 1854.

⁴⁴ "Editor's Table," *Knickerbocker*, XXVI, 580; "Editor's Table," *ibid.*, XXIX, 579 (June, 1847).

⁴⁵ Griswold to Fields quoted in Joy Bayless, *Rufus Wilmot Griswold, Poe's Literary Executor*, p. 117, 123; *The Prose Writers of America*, p. 544.

⁴⁶ *Democratic Review*, XVII, 62–66 (July, 1845).

NOTES TO CHAPTER III

YOUNG AMERICA'S THEORY OF CRITICISM

(Pages 39–53)

¹ "The Critic's Job of Work," *The Double Agent*, p. 287.

² "Criticism in America," *Democratic Review*, XV, 241 (September, 1844); "Critics and Criticism of the Nineteenth Century," *ibid.*, XV, 153 (August, 1844). Or perhaps H. L. Mencken's explanation is better: "Every now and then, a sense of the futility of their daily endeavors falling upon them, the critics of Christendom turn to a somewhat sour and depressing consideration of the nature and objects of their own craft" ("Criticism of Criticism of Criticism," *Criticism in America: Its Function and Status*, p. 176).

³ This classification is, of course, not completely reliable philosophically or historically; it is loose, opportunistic, and eclectic. But it seems to combine literary, historical, and philosophical standards in a way suited to the limited objectives of this account. I am chiefly indebted to Richard McKeon, "The Philosophical Bases of Art and Criticism," *Modern Philology*, XLI, 65–87, 129–171 (November, 1943; February, 1944); Paul Goodman, "Neo-Classicism, Platonism, and Romanticism," *Journal of Philosophy*, XXXI, 148–163 (March 15, 1934); Walter Jackson Bate, *From Classic to Romantic: Premises of Taste in Eighteenth-Century England, passim;* Austin Warren, "Literary Criticism," *Literary Scholarship*, pp. 133–174; Ernest H. Templin, "The Social Approach to Literature," *University of California Publications in Modern Philology*, XXVIII, 1–24 (June 17, 1944); William Charvat, *The Origins of American Critical Thought, 1810–1835, passim.*

⁴ J. E. Spingarn stated it thus: "To have sensations in the presence of a work of art and to express them, that is the function of Criticism for the impressionistic critic" ("The New Criticism," *Criticism in America*, p. 11).

⁵ See Charvat, *American Critical Thought*, pp. 164–165 and *passim*.

⁶ "Cornelius Mathews's Writings," *New York Review*, VII, 432 (October, 1840); "Amateur Authors and Small Critics," *Democratic Review*, XVII, 64–66 (July, 1845).

⁷ "The Poets and Poetry of America," *Democratic Review*, XI, 177–178 (August, 1842).

⁸ "Tecumseh," *ibid.*, XI, 643–644 (December, 1842). I assume this review to be O'Sullivan's purely from stylistic and thematic internal evidence—the expansive liberal rhetoric, the opposition to capital punishment, etc.

⁹ "Nature—A Prose Poem," *Democratic Review*, I, 319–320 (February, 1838); "A Disciple," "Emerson's Essays," *ibid.*, XVI, 589 (June, 1845).

¹⁰ "Miss Fuller's Papers on Literature and Art," *ibid.*, XIX, 198–202 (September, 1846); "Modern English Poets," *ibid.*, XIX, 316–320 (October, 1846); "Critics and Criticism of the Nineteenth Century," *ibid.*, XV, 162 (August, 1844); "Criticism in America," *ibid.*, XV, 249 (September, 1844).

[11] This classification of methods corresponds roughly to the classifications of intrinsic and extrinsic approaches in René Wellek and Austin Warren, *Theory of Literature*, published after my order was set down.

[12] Poe's enemy, the *Knickerbocker*, referred slurringly to his following of the old-fashioned Scotch critics and his interest in technique: Poe's criticism of poetry seems "to have been written after a very thorough cramming of BLAIR'S lectures and the essays of LORD KAIMES [*sic*]." His definition of a poem seems to be: "a poem is a metrical composition without ideas" (Literary Notice of *The Raven, and Other Poems*, XXVII, 70 [January, 1846]).

[13] *Graham's*, XX, 68–69 (January, 1842). The absence of the passage quoted from Mathews in the collected works of Poe requires one to turn to the original magazine article.

[14] "Papers on Literature and Art," *Whig Review*, IV, 514–519 (November, 1846).

[15] "Cooper's Works," *Democratic Review*, XXV, 52 (July, 1849); "Mr. Forrest's Oration," *ibid.*, III, 54 (September, 1838).

[16] See "Philosophical Chit-Chat," *Characters and Criticisms*, II, 204–213, for Jones's attitude on this point.

[17] His most detailed objection to the Scotch school is found in "The Scotch School," *Characters and Criticisms*, II, 261–264.

[18] "Critics and Criticism of the Nineteenth Century," *Democratic Review*, XV, 156 (August, 1844).

[19] On Dana's pioneering, see Charvat, *American Critical Thought*, pp. 177–180; *Whig Review*, V, 274–277 (March, 1847). Jones approved more heartily of Hazlitt partly because he was in sympathy with Hazlitt's liberal politics; Dana, as we have seen, was politically conservative.

[20] *Democratic Review*, XV, 153–162 (August, 1844), 241–249 (September, 1844).

[21] "Poets and Poetry of England," *Whig Review*, II, 39 (July, 1845). Whipple, of course, followed essentially the same method of criticism, except that his ideas were not liberal.

[22] *From Classic to Romantic*, p. 188.

NOTES TO CHAPTER IV

Young America's Theory of Literature

(Pages 54–94)

[1] Since the drama was treated almost exclusively as closet drama and as essentially another form of poetry or fiction in the *Democratic Review*, I have not separated it as a form. There was no dramatic criticism, properly speaking.

[2] For a clear summary of these basic premises see [George Allen] "Study of Works of Genius," *New York Review*, I, 161–178 (March, 1837).

[3] Merle Curti remarks an unfortunate fact in American scholarship: the reception and impact of Utilitarianism in American thought have not been systematically studied. But for a convenient summary of the connection between the liberal, reforming wing of romanticism and Utilitarianism in America see Curti's section "The Roots of Reform: Romanticism and Utilitarianism" in *The Growth of American Thought*, pp. 371–376. For a similar treatment, somewhat more full, see "Jacksonian Democracy and Literature" in Schlesinger, *Jackson*, pp. 369–390.

Notes

⁴ See *Benthamite Reviewing: The First Twelve Years of the Westminster Review, 1824–1836*, pp. 96–129, 155–163, and "Horne's New Spirit of the Age," *Democratic Review*, XV, 62 (July, 1844). One significant difference between the *Westminster* and the *Democratic* was that few of the *Westminster*'s reviews were favorable: Nesbitt explains that "the Radicals did not possess distinguished authors." The *Democratic*'s reviews were often favorable: in the United States the Democratic Radicals possessed many of the distinguished authors—or many authors who could be puffed into prominence.

⁵ *Democratic Review*, VIII, 251–271 (September, 1840); XV, 441–453 (November, 1844).

⁶ "Mrs. Hemans," *New York Review*, I, 206 (March, 1837).

⁷ "Religious Poetry (English) of the Seventeenth Century," *Whig Review*, III, 251–252 (March, 1846).

⁸ "Crabbe," *New York Review*, I, 96–109 (March, 1837).

⁹ "The Culture of the Imagination," *Arcturus*, I, 236–243 (March, 1841).

¹⁰ *Democratic Review*, I, 1–13 (October, 1837); I, 319–329 (February, 1838).

¹¹ "Mr. Forrest's Oration," *ibid.*, III, 51–55 (September, 1838).

¹² "Bryant's Poems," *ibid.*, VI, 273–286 (October, 1839); "The Great Nation of Futurity," *ibid.*, VI, 426–430 (November, 1839); "American Poetry," *ibid.*, VIII, 399–430 (November, 1840).

¹³ Letter of February 12, 1843, *Letters*, III, 146–147.

¹⁴ "Unitarian Portraits," *Democratic Review*, XV, 389–396 (October, 1844); "New Poetry in New-England," *ibid.*, XX, 396–398 (May, 1847).

¹⁵ *Democratic Review*, XI, 196–200 (August, 1842).

¹⁶ At the end of the first paragraph the reviewer wrote: "But enough: we have something to say about Petrarch, something about Campbell, and something about whatever may come in our way, but no more about this book."

¹⁷ We have here a curious direct parallel with Marxian literary criticism a hundred years later—a parallel which makes quite apparent the obvious similarities between the *Democratic*'s criticism and later Marxian criticism. William Empson, while objecting to a narrow Marxian approach, writes: "Gray's *Elegy* is an odd case of poetry with latent political ideas." It suggests, the communist would say, "that we ought to accept the injustice of society as we do the inevitability of death" (*English Pastoral Poetry*, pp. 4–5).

¹⁸ "Petrarch," *Democratic Review*, XI, 277–282 (September, 1842). This essay finds itself in an appropriate spot in the magazine: it is preceded by a contribution from Whittier and followed by one from Whitman.

¹⁹ "Devotional Poetry," *New York Review*, V, 353–355 (October, 1839); "Whipple's Essays and Reviews," *Whig Review*, IX, 266 (February, 1849); "The Progress and Disorganization," *ibid.*, II, 90–99 (July, 1845); "American Letters—Their Character and Advancement," *ibid.*, I, 575–580* (June, 1845); "Hawthorne," *ibid.*, IV, 296–316 (September, 1846).

²⁰ *Democratic Review*, XII, 158–163 (February, 1843).

²¹ *Ibid.*, XII, 392–400 (April, 1843), 479–484 (May, 1843).

²² *Ibid.*, XIII, 266–279 (September, 1843).

²³ Brownson, "Synthetic Philosophy (continued), *ibid.*, XII, 48–55 (January, 1843); [Emerson] "Mr. Channing's Poems," *ibid.*, XIII, 309–314 (September, 1843); letters of Lowell to B. G. Loring and C. F. Briggs, June 15, 1843, August 9, 1843, *Letters*, I, 71–73.

²⁴ "Female Novelists," *Democratic Review*, XIV, 489 (May, 1844).

²⁵ "The Reception of Mr. Dickens," *ibid.*, X, 315–320 (April, 1842).

[26] "Horne's New Spirit of the Age," *ibid.*, XV, 61–62 (July, 1844).

[27] *Democratic Review*, XVIII, 471–474 (June, 1846).

[28] "Cornelius Mathews's Writings," *New York Review*, VII, 430–439 (October, 1840).

[29] *Democratic Review*, XVII, 212–219 (September, 1845).

[30] "Essay" is taken here in the broad sense (of W. A. Jones below) of the essay proper and closely related forms such as the sermon, the oration, the literary address, the political pamphlet and editorial, the letter, the review article, and the—whatever one chooses to call a work like *Sartor Resartus*.

[31] "New-Old Essays of Addison and Steele," *Democratic Review*, XIV, 285–286 (March, 1844).

[32] *Essays upon Authors and Books*, pp. 13–18. Though this essay did not appear in the *Democratic Review*, Jones, a systematic plagiarist of himself, used all these ideas and some of these exact sentences in various articles in the *Review*.

[33] "Political Pamphleteering," *Democratic Review*, XI, 376–386 (October, 1842).

[34] "Political Satire and Satirists," *ibid.*, XI, 621–623 (December, 1842).

[35] "Horne's New Spirit of the Age," *ibid.*, XV, 55–58 (July, 1844).

[36] "Unitarian Portraits," *ibid.*, XV, 396 (October, 1844).

[37] "English Letter Writers," *ibid.*, XVI, 433–434 (May, 1845).

[38] "Unitarian Portraits," *ibid.*, XV, 354 (October, 1844); "On Preaching," *ibid.*, XVII, 31–39 (July, 1845).

[39] *New York Review*, V, 226–227 (July, 1839); *ibid.*, I, 447–457 (October, 1837).

[40] "American Women," *Democratic Review*, VI, 127–128 (August, 1839).

[41] [H. N. Hudson] "Whipple's Essays and Reviews," *Whig Review*, IX, 265 (February, 1849).

[42] See Benjamin T. Spencer, "A National Literature, 1837–1855," *American Literature*, VIII, 125–159 (May, 1936).

[43] *New York Review*, VII, 430–439 (October, 1840).

[44] *Democratic Review*, I, 14–15 (October, 1837).

[45] *Ibid.*, VI, 428–429 (November, 1839).

[46] "American Poetry," *ibid.*, VIII, 428–429 (November, 1840).

[47] "American Letters—Their Character and Advancement," *Whig Review*, I, 575–580* (June, 1845); "The Wisdom of Touchstone," *Alleghanian*, I, 56–58 (June 14, 1845).

[48] "Hawthorne," *Whig Review*, IV, 296–316 (September, 1846).

[49] "Nationality in Literature," *Democratic Review*, XX, 264–272 (March, 1847).

[50] This praise of Mathews points to Duyckinck as the author of the first two articles. The third is by another hand, and there is an editorial note apologizing for the praise of Mathews in the last number: the editor (no longer a Young American) "regards the estimate of this partial friend as altogether too extravagant."

[51] "Nationality in Literature," *Democratic Review*, XX, 316–320 (April, 1847); "The Prose Writers of America," *ibid.*, XX, 384–391 (May, 1847).

[52] "Cooper's Works," *ibid.*, XXV, 51–55 (July, 1849).

[53] *Benthamite Reviewing*, p. 97; "Gibbon," *Democratic Review*, XX, 524 (June, 1847). The reviewer, it should be added, was praising Gibbon in the major part of the article.

[54] "Anthon's Classical Dictionary," *Democratic Review*, IX, 133–142 (August, 1841).

[55] "Dr. Anthon and the Democratic Review," *New World*, III, 93–94 (August 7, 1841).

[56] "Anthon's Dictionary and Defence," *Democratic Review*, IX, 360–382 (October, 1841).

[57] "Children's Books," *ibid.*, XV, 537–538 (December, 1844). See also Jones's similar discussions in "Religious Novels" and "The Life and Adventures of Philip Quarll," *Boston Miscellany*, I, 214–217 (May, 1842), II, 211–215 (November, 1842).

[58] *Democratic Review*, XVI, 509–510 (May, 1845).

[59] "New Poetry in New England," *ibid.*, XX, 398 (May, 1847).

[60] "Read's Poems," *Whig Review*, X, 309–310 (September, 1849); W. B., "Uhland," *ibid.*, VII, 134–135 (February, 1848).

[61] "Festus," *ibid.*, V, 123 (February, 1847).

[62] "New Poetry in New England," *Democratic Review*, XX, 396 (May, 1847).

[63] *The Athenaeum: A Mirror of Victorian Culture*, p. 235.

NOTES TO CHAPTER V

YOUNG AMERICA'S CRITICAL JUDGMENTS

(Pages 95–121)

[1] "Sappho, and the Female Poets of Greece," *Democratic Review*, VII, 18–31 (January, 1840); "The Stars That Have Set in the Nineteenth Century. No. III.—Goethe," "No. IV.—Schiller," *ibid.*, X, 581–594 (June, 1842), XI, 34–41 (July, 1842); "Contemporary Spanish Poetry," *ibid.*, XIV, 395–408 (April, 1844).

[2] "Petrarch," *ibid.*, XI, 277–282 (September, 1842); "Petrarch," *Whig Review*, I, 468–476 (May, 1845).

[3] "Alfieri," *Democratic Review*, XV, 513–519 (November, 1844); "Pierre Jean De Béranger, His Life and Writings," *ibid.*, XXIV, 248–256 (March, 1849).

[4] *Democratic Review*, V, 489–498 (May, 1839).

[5] "Old English Literature.—George Herbert," *New York Review*, II, 111–133 (January, 1838).

[6] "Religious Poetry (English) of the Seventeenth Century," *Whig Review*, III, 250–258 (March, 1846).

[7] "Political Satire and Satirists," *Democratic Review*, XI, 621–630 (December, 1842); "Literary Physicians," *ibid.*, XIII, 595–602 (December, 1843); "English Letter Writers," *ibid.*, XVI, 443 (May, 1845).

[8] "Modern English Poets," *ibid.*, XIX, 316–320 (October, 1846); "Motherwell's Poems," *ibid.*, X, 17–24 (January, 1842).

[9] "Wordsworth's Sonnets to Liberty," *ibid.*, XII, 158–163 (February, 1843); "Wordsworth's Sonnets on the Punishment of Death," *ibid.*, X, 272–288 (March, 1842).

[10] *Shelley in America in the Nineteenth Century*, pp. 84–86; "Percy Bysshe Shelley," *Democratic Review*, XIII, 603–623 (December, 1843). Miss Power is not quite accurate, I believe, when she maintains that "it is as a literary critic, rather than as an advocate of any social creed, that Godwin approaches his subject." I should prefer to say that he was a literary critic *and* an advocate of a social creed and that it is extraordinarily difficult to separate the two functions in his article.

[11] "Miss Barrett's Poems," *Whig Review*, I, 38–48 (January, 1845); "Horne's New Spirit of the Age," *Democratic Review*, XV, 59–60 (July, 1844).

[12] Henry Norman Hudson, "Festus," *Whig Review*, V, 43–61, 123–148 (January, February, 1847); "Festus," *Democratic Review*, XVII, 454–461 (December, 1845); "Poetry for the People," *Democratic Review*, XIII, 270–274 (September, 1843).

[13] Notice of *Calaynos* by George H. Boker, *Whig Review*, IX, 105 (January, 1849); notice of *Poems* by William Thompson Bacon, *ibid.*, IX, 434 (April, 1849).

[14] "Hawthorne and His Mosses," *Literary World*, VII, 145–146 (August 24, 1850).

 [15] "Miriam," *Democratic Review,* I, 49–66 (October, 1837); "Our Neglected Poets," *ibid.,* I, 293–306, 458–476 (February, March, 1838); "Recent American Poetry," *ibid.,* V, 523–541 (June, 1839); "Bryant's Poems," *ibid.,* VI, 273–286 (October, 1839); "The Poetry of Bryant," *ibid.,* XVI, 185–191 (February, 1845); "American Poetry," *ibid.,* VIII, 399–430 (November, 1840); "The Poetry of the West," *ibid.,* IX, 23–44 (July, 1841); "Longfellow's Ballads and Poems," *ibid.,* X, 182–193 (February, 1842); "Lucy Hooper," *ibid.,* XI, 90–94 (July, 1842); "Mrs. Sigourney," *ibid.,* XI, 246–249 (September, 1842).

[16] "Mr. Mathews's 'Poems on Man,' " *ibid.,* XIII, 415–425 (October, 1843).

[17] "New Poetry in New-England," *ibid.,* XX, 392–398, XXI, 294–300 (May, October, 1847).

[18] "The Female Poets of America," *ibid.,* XXIV, 232–241 (March, 1849).

[19] "The Life and Writings of Heinrich Zschokke," *ibid.,* XVII, 25–28 (July, 1845); "The Wandering Jew," *ibid.,* XVII, 417–423 (December, 1845).

[20] "Horne's New Spirit of the Age," *ibid.,* XV, 51–55 (July, 1844).

[21] "Headlong Hall and Night-Mare Abbey," *ibid.,* XVI, 578–584 (June, 1845). For Van Doren's statement see *The Life of Thomas Love Peacock,* p. 268.

[22] "Cornelius Mathews's Writings," *New York Review,* VII, 430–439 (October, 1840); "Big Abel and the Little Manhattan," *Whig Review,* II, 532–536 (November, 1845).

[23] "Nathaniel Hawthorne," *Democratic Review,* XVI, 376–384 (April, 1845). The final phrase is an epitome of what most of the critics were seeking: "A truly pure, gentle and acceptable man of Genius." The trouble was that most geniuses had to be dead for some time before they became tractable, especially one like Poe.

[24] "Melville's Mardi," *ibid.,* XXV, 44–50 (July, 1849).

[25] "Political Theorists of the English Commonwealth," "Political Pamphleteering," "Political Satire and Satirists," *ibid.,* XI, 305–309, 376–386, 621–630 (September, October, December, 1842).

[26] "On Preaching," *ibid.,* XVII, 31–39 (July, 1845); "The Old English Pulpit," "The Old English Pulpit. No. II. Platonic Divines.—Queen Anne's Divines.—Sterne," *ibid.,* XVIII, 259–265, 344–352 (April, May, 1846).

[27] "Horne's New Spirit of the Age," *ibid.,* XV, 55–58 (July, 1844).

[28] "Criticism: Coleridge," *Whig Review,* III, 587 (June, 1846).

[29] "Critics and Criticism of the Nineteenth Century," *Democratic Review,* XV, 153–162 (August, 1844).

[30] "Unitarian Portraits," *ibid.,* XV, 389–396 (October, 1844).

[31] Notice of *The Method of Nature, New York Review,* X, 219–222 (January, 1842); "Mr. Emerson and Transcendentalism," *Whig Review,* I, 233–243 (March, 1845); "Gilfillan's Literary Portraits," *ibid.,* V, 394–396 (April, 1847).

[32] "Channing on 'Self-Culture,' " *Democratic Review,* V, 85–91 (January, 1839); "On the Elevation of the Laboring Portion of the Community," *ibid.,* VII, 529–539; VIII, 51–66 (June, July, 1840); "Dr. Channing's Recent Writings," *ibid.,* IX, 315–326 (October, 1841); "The Death of Dr. Channing," *ibid.,* XI, 561–566 (December, 1842); George Bancroft, "William Ellery Channing," *ibid.,* XII, 524–526 (May, 1843).

[33] "Hudson's Lectures on Shakespeare," *Whig Review,* VIII, 40 (July, 1848); "Unitarian Portraits," *Democratic Review,* XV, 395 (October, 1844); notice of Brownson's *The Laboring Class, New York Review,* VII, 522 (October, 1840).

[34] "Omoo," *Whig Review,* VI, 45 (July, 1847); "Shakespeare *versus* Sand," *ibid.,* V, 476–481 (May, 1847); "Hudson's Lectures on Shakespeare," *ibid.,* VIII, 44 (July, 1848).

[35] "Hawthorne and His Mosses," *Literary World,* VII, 126 (August 17, 1850).

NOTES TO CHAPTER VI

Conclusion

(Pages 122–128)

[1] "Fields," pp. 75–94; "Literary Economics and Literary History," *English Institute Essays, 1949,* pp. 73–91.

[2] "Astraea: The Balance of Illusions," *Complete Poetical Works of Oliver Wendell Holmes,* pp. 336–337; see Mathews's review of the poem in the *Literary World,* VII, 330–331 (October 26, 1850).

[3] "Capital Punishment," Brooklyn *Daily Times,* May 22, 1858, in *Uncollected Poetry and Prose of Walt Whitman,* II, 15.

[4] For the description of the literary critics before 1835 see Charvat, *American Critical Thought,* pp. 1–26.

[5] "Periodical Literature of America," *Blackwood's,* LXIII, 111–112 (January, 1848).

[6] "Tale Writing," *Complete Works,* XIII, 143–144.

BIBLIOGRAPHY

Unpublished letters, diaries, and other papers in the Duyckinck Collection at the New York Public Library have supplied important information. The Huntington Library copies of *Arcturus,* autographed by Evert A. Duyckinck, have marginal notations which identify the authors of many reviews and articles.

SOURCES

Arcturus, I–III (December, 1840–May, 1842).
Democratic Review, I–XXV (October, 1837–December, 1849). Exact title: *The United States Magazine and Democratic Review;* New Series, IX [etc.].
New York Review, I–X (March, 1837–April, 1842). Exact title: *The New York Review and Quarterly Church Journal,* first number; *The New York Review,* second number [etc.].
Whig Review, I–X (January, 1845–December, 1849). Exact title: *The American Review: A Whig Journal of Politics, Literature, Art and Science,* I–VI (1845–1847); *The American Review: A Whig Journal Devoted to Politics and Literature,* VII [etc.] (1847 et seqq.); First Series, I–VI (1845–1847); New Series, I [etc.], Whole Numbers, VII [etc.] (1848 et seqq.). The whole numbers have been used in citing this periodical.

OTHER WORKS CONSULTED

Adams, John Quincy. *Memoirs of John Quincy Adams, Comprising Portions of His Diary, from 1795 to 1848,* ed. Charles Francis Adams. 12 vols. Philadelphia: J. B. Lippincott & Co., 1874–1877.
Adkins, Nelson Frederick. *Fitz-Greene Halleck, an Early Knickerbocker Wit and Poet.* New Haven: Yale University Press, 1930.
[Anthon, Charles ?] "Dr. Anthon and the Democratic Review," *New World,* III, 93–94 (August 7, 1841).
Bate, Walter Jackson. *From Classic to Romantic: Premises of Taste in Eighteenth-Century England.* Cambridge, Mass.: Harvard University Press, 1946.
Bayless, Joy. *Rufus Wilmot Griswold, Poe's Literary Executor.* Nashville: Vanderbilt University Press, 1943.
Bigelow, John. *Retrospections of an Active Life.* Vol. I. New York: Baker & Taylor Co., 1909.
Blackmur, R. P. *The Double Agent: Essays in Craft and Elucidation.* New York: Arrow Editions, 1935.

Boynton, Henry Walcott. *Annals of American Bookselling, 1638–1850.* New York: John Wiley & Sons, 1932.

Brandes, Georg. *Main Currents in Nineteenth Century Literature,* Vol. VI: *Young Germany.* London: William Heinemann Ltd., 1923.

[Bristed, Charles Astor] "The Periodical Literature of America," *Blackwood's Edinburgh Magazine,* LXIII, 106–112 (January, 1848).

Carey, H. C. *Letters on International Copyright.* Philadelphia: A. Hart, late Carey and Hart, 1853.

Charvat, William. "James T. Fields and the Beginnings of Book Promotion, 1840–1855," *Huntington Library Quarterly,* VIII, 75–94 (November, 1944).

—— "Literary Economics and Literary History," in *English Institute Essays, 1949,* ed. Alan S. Downer. New York: Columbia University Press, 1950.

—— *The Origins of American Critical Thought, 1810–1835.* Philadelphia: University of Pennsylvania Press, 1936.

[Clark, Lewis Gaylord] "Editor's Table," *Knickerbocker,* IX, 528 (May, 1837); XXVI, 580 (December, 1845); XXVIII, 451 (November, 1846); XXIX, 579 (June, 1847).

Curti, Merle E. "George N. Sanders—American Patriot of the Fifties," *South Atlantic Quarterly,* XXVII, 79–87 (January, 1928).

—— *The Growth of American Thought.* New York: Harper & Brothers, 1943.

—— "The Reputation of America Overseas (1776–1860)," *American Quarterly,* I, 81–82 (Spring, 1949).

—— " 'Young America,' " *American Historical Review,* XXXII, 34–55 (October, 1926).

Dictionary of American Biography. 22 vols. New York: Charles Scribner's Sons, 1928–1944.

[Duyckinck, Evert A. ?] "Sketches of American Prose Writers. No. 1. William A. Jones," *Broadway Journal,* I, 28 (January 11, 1845).

Emerson, Ralph Waldo, and Henry David Thoreau. "The Emerson-Thoreau Correspondence," ed. F. B. Sanborn, *Atlantic Monthly,* LXIX, 577–596 (May, 1892).

—— *The Complete Works of Ralph Waldo Emerson,* ed. Edward Waldo Emerson. Centenary Edition. 12 vols. Boston: Houghton, Mifflin and Company, 1903–1904.

—— *The Letters of Ralph Waldo Emerson,* ed. Ralph L. Rusk. 6 vols. New York: Columbia University Press, 1939.

Empson, William. *English Pastoral Poetry.* New York: W. W. Norton & Co., 1938.

[Godwin, Parke] "Prospectus," *Pathfinder,* I, 30 (March 4, 1843).

Goodman, Paul. "Neo-Classicism, Platonism, and Romanticism," *Journal of Philosophy*, XXXI, 148–163 (March 15, 1934).

Goodspeed, George T. "The Home Library," *Papers of the Bibliographical Society of America*, XLII, 110–118 (1948).

Goodrich, S. G. *Recollections of a Lifetime*. New York: Arundel Print, 1856.

Griswold, Rufus Wilmot. *Passages from the Correspondence and Other Papers of Rufus W. Griswold*. Cambridge, Mass.: W. M. Griswold, 1898.

—— *The Prose Writers of America*. Philadelphia: Carey and Hart, 1847.

Harper, J. Henry. *The House of Harper: A Century of Publishing in Franklin Square*. New York: Harper & Brothers, 1912.

Hawthorne, Julian. *Nathaniel Hawthorne and His Wife*. 2 vols. Boston: Houghton Mifflin Company, 1884.

Hawthorne, Nathaniel. *The American Notebooks*, ed. Randall Stewart. New Haven: Yale University Press, 1932.

Hofstadter, Richard. "William Leggett, Spokesman of Jacksonian Democracy," *Political Science Quarterly*, LVIII, 581–594 (December, 1943).

Holmes, Oliver Wendell. *The Complete Poetical Works of Oliver Wendell Holmes*. Cambridge Edition. Boston: Houghton, Mifflin and Company, 1895.

Jarrell, Randall. "Contemporary Poetry Criticism," *New Republic*, CV, 88–90 (July 21, 1941).

Jones, William Alfred. *Characters and Criticisms*. 2 vols. New York: I. Y. Westervelt, 1857.

—— *Essays upon Authors and Books*. New York: N. N. Stanford, 1849.

—— "The Life and Adventures of Philip Quarll," *Boston Miscellany*, II, 211–215 (November, 1842).

[——] *Memorial of the Late Honorable David S. Jones. With an Appendix, Containing Notices of the Jones Family, of Queen's County*. New York: Stanford and Swords, 1849.

—— "Religious Novels," *Boston Miscellany*, I, 214–217 (May, 1842).

Lathrop, George Parsons. *A Study of Hawthorne*. Boston: J. R. Osgood and Company, 1876.

Lehmann-Haupt, Hellmut, in collaboration with Ruth Shephard Granniss and Lawrence C. Wroth. *The Book in America: A History of the Making, the Selling, and the Collecting of Books in the United States*. New York: R. R. Bowker Company, 1939.

Literary Notice of *The Raven, and Other Poems*, *Knickerbocker*, XXVII, 70 (January, 1846).

Lowell, James Russell. "Letters of James Russell Lowell, 1843–1854," *Bulletin of the New York Public Library*, IV, 339–345 (October, 1900).

———— *Letters of James Russell Lowell,* ed. Charles Eliot Norton. 2 vols. New York: Harper & Brothers, 1894.

McKeon, Richard. "The Philosophical Bases of Art and Criticism," *Modern Philology,* XLI, 65–87, 129–171 (November, 1943; February, 1944).

"The Magazines," *Broadway Journal,* I, 93–94 (February 8, 1845).

Mansfield, Luther Stearns. "Glimpses of Herman Melville's Life in Pittsfield, 1850–1851: Some Unpublished Letters of Evert A. Duyckinck," *American Literature,* IX, 26–48 (March, 1937).

———— "Melville's Comic Articles on Zachary Taylor," *American Literature,* IX, 411–418 (January, 1938).

Marchand, Leslie A. *The Athenaeum: A Mirror of Victorian Culture.* Chapel Hill: University of North Carolina Press, 1941.

[Mathews, Cornelius] Review of Holmes's "Astraea," *Literary World,* VII, 330–331 (October 26, 1850).

[————] "Several Days in Berkshire," *Literary World,* VII, 166 (August 31, 1850).

"Meeting of the Mutual Admiration Society," *John-Donkey,* I, 222 (April 1, 1848).

[Melville, Herman] "Hawthorne and His Mosses," *Literary World,* VII, 125–127, 145–147 (August 17, 24, 1850).

———— *Representative Selections,* ed. Willard Thorp. American Writers Series. New York: American Book Company, 1938.

Miller, Harold P. "Hawthorne Surveys His Contemporaries," *American Literature,* XII, 228–235 (May, 1940).

Mott, Frank Luther. *A History of American Magazines.* Vol. I. Cambridge, Mass.: Harvard University Press, 1938.

———— *Golden Multitudes: The Story of Best Sellers in the United States.* New York: Macmillan Co., 1947.

Nesbitt, George L. *Benthamite Reviewing: The First Twelve Years of the Westminster Review, 1824–1836.* New York: Columbia University Press, 1934.

"The New York Press," *New-York Mirror,* III, 46 (October 25, 1845).

"Notes about Men of Note," *Aristidean,* I, 153–155 (April, 1845).

Osgood, Samuel. *Evert Augustus Duyckinck, His Life, Writings and Influence.* Boston: D. Clapp & Son, 1879.

Poe, Edgar Allan. *Complete Works...* Edited by James A. Harrison. Virginia Edition. 17 vols. New York: T. Y. Crowell & Company, 1902.

[————] "The Democratic Review," *Broadway Journal,* II, 168–169 (September 20, 1845).

[————] "Exordium," *Graham's Magazine,* XX, 68–69 (January, 1842).

[————] "Our Magazine Literature," *New World,* VI, 302–303 (March 11, 1843).

Power, Julia. *Shelley in America in the Nineteenth Century: His Relation to American Critical Thought and His Influence.* University of Nebraska Studies, XL. Lincoln: University of Nebraska Press, 1940.

Pratt, Julius W. "John L. O'Sullivan and Manifest Destiny," *New York History*, XIV, 214–234 (July, 1933).

—— "The Origin of 'Manifest Destiny,'" *American Historical Review*, XXXII, 795–798 (July, 1927).

Procter, Page S., Jr. "William Leggett (1801–1839): Journalist and Literator," *Papers of the Bibliographical Society of America*, XLIV, 239–253 (1950).

Putnam, George Palmer. *American Facts.* London: Wiley & Putnam, 1845.

Roorbach, Orville A., comp. *Bibliotheca Americana.* New York: published by the compiler, October, 1852.

Sanborn, F. B. *Hawthorne and His Friends.* Cedar Rapids, Iowa: Torch Press, 1908.

[Sanders, George N.] "Fogy Literature," *Democratic Review*, XXX, 396–400 (May, 1852).

Schlesinger, Arthur M., Jr. *The Age of Jackson.* Boston: Little, Brown and Company, 1945.

Spencer, Benjamin T. "A National Literature, 1837–1855," *American Literature*, VIII, 125–159 (May, 1936)

Sumner, George. "Letters of George Sumner, 1837–1844," *Proceedings of the Massachusetts Historical Society*, XLVI, 341–370 (March, 1913).

Templin, Ernest H. "The Social Approach to Literature," *University of California Publications in Modern Philology*, XXVIII, 1–24 (June 17, 1944).

Thoreau, Henry David. *Familiar Letters of Henry David Thoreau*, ed. F. B. Sanborn. The Writings of Henry David Thoreau, XI. Boston: Houghton Mifflin Company, 1894.

Trimble, William. "Diverging Tendencies in New York Democracy in the Period of the Loco-Focos," *American Historical Review*, XXIV, 396–421 (April, 1919).

—— "The Social Philosophy of the Loco-Foco Democracy," *American Journal of Sociology*, XXVI, 705–715 (May, 1921).

Van Doren, Carl. *The Life of Thomas Love Peacock.* London: J. M. Dent & Sons, 1911.

Warren, Austin. "Literary Criticism," in *Literary Scholarship*, ed. Norman Foerster. Chapel Hill: University of North Carolina Press, 1941.

Wellek, René, and Austin Warren, *Theory of Literature.* New York: Harcourt, Brace and Company [c. 1949].

Whitman, Walt. "Capital Punishment," Brooklyn *Daily Times*, May 22, 1858, in *The Uncollected Poetry and Prose of Walt Whitman*, collected and edited by Emory Holloway. 2 vols. Garden City, N.Y.: Doubleday, Page & Company, 1921.

Wilson, James Grant. *The Life and Letters of Fitz-Greene Halleck.* New York: D. Appleton and Co., 1869.

"The Wisdom of Touchstone," *Alleghanian,* I, 56–58 (June 14, 1843).

Wright, Lyle H. "A Statistical Survey of American Fiction, 1774–1850," *Huntington Library Quarterly,* II, 309–318 (April, 1939).

——— comp. *American Fiction, 1774–1850: A Contribution toward a Bibliography.* Huntington Library Publications. San Marino, Calif.: [Huntington Library] 1939.

INDEX